W9-CKH-518

THEIR FINEST HOUR

Profiles of America's Veterans

THE
DONNING COMPANY
PUBLISHERS

The Donning Company Publishers
184 Business Park Drive, Suite 206
Virginia Beach, VA 23462

Steve Mull, General Manager
Barbara Buchanan, Office Manager
Heather L. Floyd, Editor
Chad Harper Casey, Graphic Designer
Kathy Adams, Imaging Artist
Lori Porter, Project Research Coordinator
Tonya Washam, Marketing Specialist
Pamela Engelhard, Marketing Advisor

Dennis Walton, Project Director

Library of Congress Cataloging-in-Publication Data

Millett, Wesley, 1939-
Their finest hour : profiles of America's veterans / author, Wesley Millett.
pages cm
"American Veterans Center and World War II Veterans Committee."
ISBN 978-1-57864-811-5 (hardcover : alk. paper)
1. Veterans--United States--Biography. 2. United States--Armed Forces--Biography. I. American Veterans Center. II. World War II Veterans Committee. III. Title.
U52.M58 2012
355.0092'273--dc23
2012050762

Printed in the United States of America at Walsworth Publishing Company

THEIR FINEST HOUR

Profiles of America's Veterans

American Veterans Center and World War II Veterans Committee

Foreword General P. X. Kelley ★ **Preface** Tim Holbert ★ **Introduction** James C. Roberts
Author Wesley Millett ★ **Editor** Tim Holbert

TABLE OF CONTENTS

FOREWORD

Throughout my 37 years of active-duty service in the Marine Corps and years of retirement since, I have been privileged to meet many thousands of Americans who have worn the uniform in service to our country. Each one of them, no matter their background, their rank, or their decorations, has a story to tell.

For veterans, our military service plays a defining role in our lives, whether we make a career of it or not. Our service teaches us discipline, provides us with a sense of honor, and gives us the opportunity to know that we have each served something larger than ourselves.

Because each veteran's service is so much a part of them, and so valuable to our nation, it is vitally important that their stories are preserved, so that future generations can learn from them, and future leaders can follow their example.

This book is intended to play a small part in preserving just a few of these stories. These are ordinary Americans who, through fate, found themselves in extraordinary circumstances and rose to the challenges presented before them. Some distinguished themselves through combat, some by being pioneers and leaders, and some by stepping up to serve when few might have expected them to feel the need to do so. All profiled here—as all who have served honorably—can be very proud of their service.

Preserving and sharing stories like these, and of all veterans, is part of the mission of the American Veterans Center. The mission remains vitally important, as respect and honor for those who have served is necessary to ensure future generations who will endeavor to follow in their footsteps. As General George Washington noted, "The willingness with which our young people are likely to serve in any war, no matter how justified, shall be directly proportional to how they perceive veterans of early wars were treated and appreciated by our nation." It is our duty to make sure that our veterans' stories of valor, sacrifice, and honor are preserved and appreciated, long after they have hung up their uniforms and have left this earth.

General P. X. Kelley (USMC-Ret.)
28th Commandant of the United States Marine Corps

PREFACE

Shortly after becoming prime minister of the United Kingdom following the fall of France and the Nazi domination of Continental Europe in 1940, Winston Churchill delivered a speech before the House of Commons in which he asserted that when future historians looked at Britain, the coming moment at which they stood up to the overwhelming German power would be seen as "their finest hour."

Service in wartime tests the honor, valor, integrity, loyalty, and dedication of all who battle. Every man and woman who serves has a story, no matter how seemingly great or small. And for each who serves honorably, the tests they face are, for them, indeed "their finest hour."

In *Their Finest Hour*, we are honored to share the stories of veterans from World War II to the present day who have risen to the challenges presented before them during wartime. These are everyday men and women from across America who found themselves in extraordinary situations, and rose to the occasion. Some are highly decorated, some are not, but all made an impact on our military's history through their service. Like all American veterans, they served for something larger than themselves. And like all veterans who served honorably, they should be forever thanked for their service.

The mission of the American Veterans Center and the World War II Veterans Committee is to guard the legacy and honor the sacrifice of American veterans of every generation. Each of the veterans profiled in this book was interviewed for our weekly radio series, *Veterans Chronicles*, airing nationwide weekly on the Radio America network. Additionally, the Center publishes *American Valor Quarterly*, the nation's only magazine dedicated solely to firsthand accounts from veterans and active-duty service members who have served in the defining moments in American military history.

In addition to guarding the history of our veterans, the American Veterans Center honors their sacrifice by connecting our veterans to students and young people who are the future leaders of our country, as well as producing documentary and television programming honoring the stories of our veterans. The Center produces the National Memorial Day Parade, our nation's largest Memorial Day event, bringing together more than 300,000 spectators to Constitution Avenue in Washington, DC, annually, with a national television audience of several million across the country. *The Wounded Warrior Experience* is an annual television program featuring wounded service members sharing their own stories, with resource information for their fellow service members experiencing similar situations. Our newest program, *The American Veterans Center Awards*, honors American heroes, both heralded and unsung, for their service and is the first awards show in the nation to honor those who deserve it most: our veterans.

We hope that you enjoy *Their Finest Hour*, and that you will join us in our mission of preserving our veterans' stories and legacies. You can learn more about the American Veterans Center and World War II Veterans Committee by visiting www.americanveteranscenter.org and www.wwiivets.com.

Tim Holbert
Executive Director
American Veterans Center

INTRODUCTION

It is my privilege to introduce to you this volume titled *Their Finest Hour* within which are chronicled the stories of sixty-one veterans interviewed by the American Veterans Center (AVC) over the past ten years. These accounts reflect combat experiences spanning almost a century of military service to our country, from that of the late Frank Buckles, our last surviving World War I veteran who served in Europe in 1917 to 1919, to that of the generation that has most recently served in Iraq and Afghanistan.

The veterans profiled in this book represent a broad variety of ethnic groups, races, religions, and economic and social backgrounds—all threads in the amazing American tapestry. Despite their differences, however, all of these veterans had one thing in common—that in times of national peril, they answered their country's call.

At the American Veterans Center, it is our mission, and our privilege, to preserve the legacy of our veterans for current and future generations. We do this through a wide variety of programs, including the recording of video and audio oral history interviews which we conduct in partnership with the Veterans History Project of the Library of Congress. Many of these oral histories are then edited for streaming on the AVC website and for television and radio broadcast.

At the American Veterans Center, *every* day is Veterans Day, and for my colleagues and me, our work is more a cause than a job.

Iraq war veteran Major Chuck Larson wrote a book titled *Heroes Among Us*. At the AVC, we are truly surrounded by heroes. It is an honor to work at a place where we make the acquaintance of heroes on practically a daily basis. These veterans come into our studios modest and humble and tell their stories in a matter-of-fact way. They are nothing special, almost all of them say. They were just doing their jobs.

Yet they are special—the finest men and women of their generations.

They fought—and in many cases bled—for the country they love. Many still bear the physical scars of their service. For others the scars are invisible, yet they are just as real nonetheless.

Many of these veterans paid a high personal price to defend America. Many of their comrades paid the ultimate price. These veterans embody values—duty, patriotism, service, sacrifice, courage, and love—that we need to recognize and instill in our young people.

I hope you find these stories as inspirational as I do, and that you will draw from them increased devotion to the country which they served so courageously.

James C. Roberts
President
American Veterans Center

★★★★★ VETERANS' STORIES

LAST LINE OF DEFENSE AT TARIN KOWT

JASON AMERINE Veteran

"As we're directing the air strikes, the townspeople came out and fought off the Taliban that made it to the city. You had old men, young men. You had children. You even had women. By about noon, the Taliban were in full retreat."

Jason Amerine, on defending Tarin Kowt against an assault by 500 to 1,000 Taliban with nine U.S. Special Forces soldiers and the townspeople, from an interview with *Veterans Chronicles*

November 17, 2001. The reconnaissance report came through at 0200 (2:00 a.m.). The Taliban were on their way to Tarin Kowt in the Orüzgān province of Afghanistan. About 500 to 1,000 insurgents were jammed into a hodgepodge of vehicles, as many as 100 or more, from pickups to large trucks. A number of them had been fitted with artillery and anti-aircraft guns. Moving quickly, Captain Jason Amerine led his Special Forces team, along with a few dozen men belonging to freedom fighter Hamid Karzai, south from Tarin Kowt, the capital of Orüzgān, to take up positions on a mountain plateau overlooking a pass from which they could intercept the Taliban convoy.

The prospects of turning back the enemy with the nine Green Berets of ODA (Operational Detachment A) 574, and with whatever help they could get from Karzai's men, was slim, but with a forward air controller overhead coordinating air support, Amerine was hopeful that he could not only stop the Taliban, but also wipe them out. If he didn't, his unit would be overrun and the town would be in the hands of the insurgents.

With the detachment waiting on the plateau above as the enemy entered the valley, Amerine unleashed his attack, devastating the convoy from both the ground and the air. Noise and confusion reigned as artillery shells, bombs, and automatic weapons fire rained down on the insurgents, causing them to disperse from the target area.

The problem was that the enemy weren't the only ones to panic. Amerine turned to see what the shouting and roaring of engines behind him was all about. The ferocity of the Navy F-18 air strikes had unnerved the Afghan fighters and they were leaving… which meant that Amerine's unit—even if it was able to hold off the Taliban—would be stranded. As a result, Amerine had to leave with Karzai's men, pick up new vehicles in Tarin Kowt, and return to intercept the enemy.

Meanwhile, the Taliban began to regroup.

Amerine was raised in Honolulu, Hawaii, where his interest in the military was encouraged by a Special Forces instructor after he joined an ROTC program at age 14 in high school. At West Point, Amerine majored in Arabic and Spanish and eventually became more or less competent in speaking five languages. As a second lieutenant, Amerine volunteered for Ranger School, and after graduating, was assigned to the 5th Battalion, 87th Infantry, which was stationed in Panama. He then joined the Joint Security Force Company at Pan Mun Jom in Korea doing DMZ (demilitarized zone) patrols.

Back in the U.S. for an advanced course, Amerine was promoted to captain. "I elected for Special Forces Assessment Selection," Amerine remarked, “where they basically try to kill you for about three weeks, and if you endure it, then they accept you for the Special Forces training.”

After being stationed at Fort Campbell in Tennessee and a stint in Kuwait, he was assigned command of two Special Forces teams, ODA 572 and ODA 574, in which he and his unit trained Kazakhstan paratroopers. “We were really teaching counterinsurgency skills to the Kazakhs,” who were fighting a Taliban organization called the Islamic Movement of Uzbekistan.

Then 9/11 happened, and after being sent back to the U.S. for last-minute training and equipping, Amerine’s outfit soon found itself in Pakistan, where it infiltrated Afghanistan west of Tarin Kowt and linked up with the forces of Hamid Karzai.

Back in the town, Amerine convinced Karzai to let him have the trucks, but by the time the unit returned to intercept the enemy, the Taliban were through the pass and approaching the last line of defense for Tarin Kowt.

As the situation began to look hopeless, armed townspeople arrived on the scene, and after several hours of close combat, Amerine’s Special Forces unit held. The Taliban were driven off, and as they scattered back toward the pass, just about all of the enemy vehicles were decimated by repeated air strikes.

Over the next several weeks, ODA 574 interdicted numerous Taliban convoys, the combined efforts of Karzai’s freedom fighters and Amerine’s Special Forces troops ultimately leading to the captures of Taliban strongholds and the surrender of Kandahar. Amerine was later hit by friendly fire from a bomber.

After recovering, he completed his master’s degree in international affairs with a major in national security at Texas A&M, and afterwards joined the faculty as an assistant professor of international relations at West Point.

Jason Amerine and his wife Brandi Michelle reside in Arlington, Virginia.

Lieutenant Colonel Jason L. Amerine

FOUR BOGEYS, FIVE O'CLOCK HIGH!

CLARENCE ANDERSON Veteran

"I got into a really hairy dogfight in the spring of '44, May 27th. We were attacked by four airplanes. It was eventually one-on-one, and an Me-109 actually got on my tail."

Bud Anderson, on being attacked by Luftwaffe fighters while escorting Allied bombers, from an interview with *Veterans Chronicles*

You couldn't tell at first. They were just four dots in the sky, and way back. But they closed quickly and were clearly German fighters. Messerschmitts, also known as Me-109s.

Clarence "Bud" Anderson knew that an Me-109 in the hands of a good pilot couldn't be taken for granted against his P-51 Mustang. Its reputation as a killing machine was well deserved.

The Me-109s swooped down and passed by as Anderson and the other Mustangs with him turned hard to the right and began to climb, the two enemies turning in tighter and tighter circles, each seeking to come up behind the other. "Our throttles were wide open, 30,000 feet up," recalled Anderson. The Mustang was a little faster than the smaller German fighters, and a little more nimble. But not by much. And according to Anderson, "These guys wanted to hang around."

For Anderson, flying for the military was an easy transition from civilian life. He had joined the Civilian Pilot Training Program (CPTP) and had gotten his pilot's license while still in college "for the price of $9.50 for an insurance policy for my folks and their written permission." He explained, "I learned to fly on a 40-horsepower Piper Cub. It had a tail skid, balloon tires, no brakes, no radio." Born in Oakland, California, on January 13, 1922, Anderson was raised on a small farm in Newcastle, went to high school in Auburn, seven miles away, and at 20, attended Sacramento Junior College, a technical school which qualified him to be an aircraft mechanic. After graduation, he went to work at the nearby Sacramento Air Depot, crating up P-40s and changing fuel cells in B-17s.

Then came Pearl Harbor, and a month later, still 20, he signed up and was off to Higley Field in Arizona, where he got his uniform and did a little marching. He eventually began his basic training at Bakersfield, California, graduating from the flying school there in

"Old Crow," the P-51 Mustang that Bud Anderson flew to become a triple-ace during World War II.

September 1942. Having received his wings and commission as a second lieutenant, Anderson was deployed to England and assigned to the newly formed 357th Fighter Group.

After further training back in Nevada, in November 1943, Anderson was on the *Queen Elizabeth* with 15,000 other troops, headed back to England, as the buildup commenced for the invasion of Normandy. The 357th Fighter Group became part of the 8th Air Force, and Anderson was soon flying combat missions in P-51s over Germany. He was now on his way to becoming a "triple ace" in the fight to clear the skies of German aircraft.*

In the dogfight with the Me-109s, Anderson was dealing with a tenacious enemy, each trying to get the upper hand; but after a while, the German pilots began to sense that things weren't going well against the faster and more agile Mustangs. They rolled out and fled east, Anderson and the others hot on their tails. As Anderson wrote in his book, *To Fly and Fight, Memoirs of a Triple Ace*, "I closed within 250 yards of the nearest Messerschmitt… and squeezed the trigger on the control stick." He continued, "I'm going like hell now, and I can see the bullets tearing at the Messerschmitt's wing root and fuselage." After Anderson poured another burst into it, pieces started falling off the plane, and it began to belch smoke as it plummeted to the ground. It was Anderson's sixth kill.

In all, of the four Me-109s that attacked the Mustangs that day, three were shot down, two by Anderson. One got away.

Nicknamed "Old Crow" by Anderson for reasons not entirely clear (he's mentioned three possibilities: the bird, the whiskey, and according to his wife… her), his P-51D carried him safety through 116 missions, engaging the Germans some 40 times and destroying 16.25 planes in the air and one on the ground. Not once was he hit by enemy aircraft. Chuck Yeager, his friend and fellow pilot of the 357th Fighter Group, called Anderson "the best fighter I ever saw." Anderson received the Legion of Merit twice and the Distinguished Flying Cross five times, as well as numerous other awards.

After 30 years of continuous military service, including a stint as a test pilot at Wright Field, Ohio, Anderson retired as a colonel in March 1972. He became manager of McDonnell Aircraft Company's Flight Test Facility at Edwards Air Force Base in California, and has been inducted into the National Aviation Hall of Fame. He has flown more than 130 different types of aircraft and logged over 7,500 flying hours.

Bud Anderson married Eleanor Cosby of Auburn, California, where they currently live.

Colonel Clarence E. Anderson

* An "ace" is a pilot who has achieved at least five victories. A "triple ace" would have 15 or more.

CLEARING A HOUSE FULL OF INSURGENTS

DAVID BELLAVIA Veteran

"April 2004 was the height of the Shia uprising, and I just happened to be in Iraq during the Najaf fight, the Mosul fight, the Baghdad fight, the Fallujah fight, the Diyala fight. Our unit was there when it was needed."

David Bellavia, on the battles he fought in while serving in Iraq, from an interview with *Veterans Chronicles*

November 10, 2004. In the heat of the fight, Staff Sergeant David Bellavia panicked and ran from the house.

His platoon in the 2nd Squad of Company A had been ordered during Operation Phantom Fury to clear a block of 12 buildings in Fallujah, Iraq, from which the jihadists—known as AIFs (Anti-Iraq Forces)—were firing at American soldiers patrolling the streets. Bellavia had gone from house to house with the others in the platoon, collecting AK-47s and other weapons, but at the tenth house, when they suddenly encountered a number of the enemy holed up and he found himself low on ammunition, he ran out the door and into the middle of the street.

But, he knew he had to go back. The men in his platoon depended on him to do his job, and some of them were already inside. Gathering his courage, Bellavia and a fellow sergeant forced themselves across the threshold and into the house. The soldier with him immediately took a hit in the shoulder, which spurred Bellavia into action. He shot an AIF preparing to fire an RPG (rocket-propelled grenade), and then turned his gun on a second insurgent, wounding him in the shoulder. Entering a bedroom, Bellavia sprayed the room with a burst of gunfire, and seeing that the wounded insurgent had followed

The Second Battle of Fallujah, which raged from November 7 to December 23, 2004, is considered the most intense battle of the war in Iraq, and is often compared to the Battle of Hue City in Vietnam for the ferocity of its urban combat.

behind him, he turned and killed him. He then took out a third AIF, shooting at him from upstairs, and when a closet in the bedroom suddenly opened and out jumped an insurgent, Bellavia managed to wound him. The jihad escaped up the stairs and Bellavia ran up after him, slipping on the blood on the stairs as he did, a bullet ripping into the wall above his head.

Following the footsteps to a bedroom on the left at the top of the stairs, Bellavia tossed a fragmentation grenade into the room. As he turned into the bedroom, he saw that it was filled with propane tanks and plastic explosives, which miraculously had not been set off by the concussion of his grenade. The insurgent, though wounded, was still very much alive. Afraid to shoot his M-16 because of what was stored in the room, Bellavia started swinging at the man with the rifle, and they were soon wrestling on the floor, the insurgent punching Bellavia in the head and kicking him in the crotch. It was a fight that would end in the death of one of them.

Bellavia had joined the Army to toughen up. "I thought the only institution I could join, the only job I could get that would give me the building blocks of what it would take to grow up," he has said, "would be the United States military." Born in Buffalo, New York, Bellavia attended high school in Lyndonville, New York, about an hour north of the city. While still in high school, he also attended a community college, taking night classes, and later graduated from Franklin Pierce College in Rindge, New Hampshire.

Bellavia enlisted in the Army in August 1999 and was sent to Fort Benning in Georgia for basic training. While at Fort Benning, he went on to the Ranger Indoctrination Program, the Bradley Crew Member School, and the TOW Missile Course. After being promoted to sergeant, he was sent to Vilseck, Germany, and from there, he was assigned as a machine gunner to Company A, Task Force 2/2, 1st Infantry Division and deployed for nine months to Kosovo, which didn't provide the action he was seeking. "You're pretty much guarding chicken coops and holding the hands of children while they wait for the bus," he recalled.

But Iraq was on the horizon. And finally, in February 2004, Bellavia found himself there, fighting jihadists in such cities as Baghdad, Mosul, and Najaf and in the Diyala Province. At no time was his life more on the line, though, than it was during the hand-to-hand combat on the second floor of the house in Fallujah. Finally, after exchanging blows with the insurgent and struggling to get the upper hand, Bellavia managed to pull out his Gerber knife and stick it into the man's throat near his collarbone and held it there until he died.

Staff Sergeant David G. Bellavia

But he wasn't done. All totaled, Bellavia took out five insurgents in the house that day, essentially saving three squads of his platoon from being wiped out.

After serving for six years, Bellavia retired from the Army with the rank of staff sergeant in 2005. In civilian life, he became vice chairman of Vets for Freedom, an author, and a candidate for political office.

David Bellavia and his wife Deanna reside in Batavia, New York.

ENEMY ATTACK IN THE APENNINES

LELAND BRISSIE Veteran

"The first round they fired was a fair distance from us. The trucks stopped and everyone started to get out. The next shell hit right at my feet. I could not see the left foot."

Lou Brissie, on the German bombardment that almost cost him his professional baseball career, from an interview with *Veterans Chronicles*

The truck slammed on its brakes and the men quickly piled out. But it was too late. The first shell had landed a distance away, warning the men of the 351st Regiment, 2nd Battalion of the 88th Infantry Division that the German artillery had them in their sights. It was December 7, 1944, and Allied forces had been slugging it out with the enemy from one crest to the next in the Northern Apennine Mountains of Italy.

This was supposed to be a day of rest for Corporal Lou Brissie and G Company. Another unit had taken over their listening post so the exhausted men could get a shower and a change of clothes, along with a hot breakfast, and now they were heading back.

Soldiers of the 88th Infantry Division march down the street in Gorizia, Italy, 1945.

The second shell exploded at the feet of Brissie. "I crawled into a creek bed, and got part way through it. I was trying to get up against the bank for shelter. I got halfway up, rolled over on my back. I could see my right foot and the hole in the boot. But I couldn't see my left foot."

Most everyone else in the squad—eight enlisted men and three of its four officers—were killed during the ensuing barrage.

Brissie collapsed and was left for dead in the snow and mud before being found unconscious a few hours later. The next thing he remembered was a chaplain kneeling over him in the aide station. Taken to a field hospital, he was told that his leg would probably need to be amputated, to which he told them, "I am a ballplayer, and I can't play if I don't have my legs." Brissie's left tibia and shinbone had been shattered by the shrapnel into 30 pieces. Saving the leg would take a miracle… and a doctor willing to try.

For Lou Brissie, playing baseball was second only to fighting for his country. Born in Anderson, South Carolina, he was raised in Greenville and in Ware Shoals, where the six-foot, four-and-one-half-inch-tall lefthander played for the Riegel Company baseball team. He was only 14 at the time. By 16, he was already fielding offers from major league baseball teams. He ended up signing with the Philadelphia Athletics after graduating from high school, the deal being that he could attend Presbyterian College for three years and then report to the Athletics.

Then the war came along, and Brissie was determined to join the Army. So he coasted through college for a couple of years and enlisted at 18 in December 1942. He went through basic training and was stationed at Camp Croft, South Carolina, where he pitched for the base team.

In the second half of 1944, Brissie was shipped overseas and was with the 88th Infantry when it began its November push into northern Italy against German divisions lodged in the Apennine Mountains. Combat was brutal, as the enemy contested every jagged peak and rocky ridge in the mountain chain. Entire platoons were annihilated by German mortars and deadly machine gun fire.

For Brissie, the war was over. After two years, 23 major operations, and 40 blood transfusions, he clung to the hope that he could play ball professionally. He credits the saving of his legs to a doctor at the Army hospital in Naples, Italy. "When I woke up late in the afternoon and I looked down and saw those 'two lumps' at the bottom of the bed, I knew I still had my legs." The road back would be long and hard, but there was at least a chance he might eventually catch on with a major league team.

Finally, he got his opportunity on September 28, 1947, when he took the mound for the Philadelphia Athletics, thanks to the willingness of manager Connie Mack to give him a chance and a contract. He pitched for seven seasons in the major leagues, wearing a special metal brace on his leg. In total, he won 44 games and saved 29. He finished fourth in the vote for the Rookie of the Year Award in 1948, and he pitched in the 1949 All Star Game. Brissie's best year was probably in 1951 for the Cleveland Indians with a 3.20 ERA in 54 games. He retired from baseball in 1953.

Corporal Leland V. Brissie

Following his career in baseball, Brissie became the national director for American Legion Baseball, and afterwards, was a scout first for the Los Angeles Dodgers and then for the Milwaukee Braves. Moving from baseball to private industry, he worked for a time as a representative for United Merchants and Manufacturers before ending his work career with the South Carolina Board of Technical Education.

Lou Brissie resides with his wife Diana in North Augusta, South Carolina.

DECOY IN THE SKIES OF NORTH VIETNAM

JACKSEL BROUGHTON Veteran

"One wingman and myself managed to corner 16 MiGs one day, and we survived the encounter. In fact, I think we dinged them up a bit, did better than they did."

Jack Broughton, on encountering the faster MiG jets while flying America's first jet aircraft, Lockheed P-80s, from an interview with *Veterans Chronicles*

May 13, 1967. The squadron of F-105 Thunderbirds, popularly known as "Thuds" by the flight crews, took off from Takhli Air Force Base in central Thailand, headed for the rail yards at Hanoi. Leading the squadron was Colonel Jack Broughton, vice commander of the 355th Tactical Fighter Wing. The task he took on for himself during the mission was to draw the fire of the 85mm and 100mm guns protecting the yards and suppress them, so the fighter-bombers behind him could then take out the targets without concern for being hit by flak.

After a successful strike on the enemy artillery, Broughton moved on to a valley nearby, where he discovered targets overlooked by intelligence. But as the squadron regrouped to begin its attack, Broughton's plane took a hit that knocked out his stability control system. Somehow, he managed to nurse the plane back to the base. There, the tail section of his aircraft was replaced during the night, and with a couple of hours of sleep, he and his pilots were in the air before dawn, buffeted by violent thunderstorms and turbulence in the pitch black as they winged their way back to the valley. Broughton's role would again be that of flak suppression.

United States Air Force F-105 Thunderbirds fly in formation.

Pulling up after an initial run, in which he had again successfully knocked out enemy artillery, Broughton noticed an undamaged building and returned to attack it, but took a hit from a SAM (surface-to-air missile) that set the plane on fire and damaged his two main hydraulic systems. The pressure of the remaining system was fluctuating badly—from zero to 3,000 pounds—

and the prospect of keeping the burning plane in the air was grim.

Broughton had been on tough operations before in a military career that extended from the end of World War II through 114 missions in Korea and, before he was reassigned, 102 missions in Vietnam. Born in Utica, New York, Broughton attended Brighton High School in Rochester, New York, and afterward gained an appointment to the United States Military Academy. He was commissioned into the U.S. Army Air Force in June 1945 and received his flight training at Garner Field, Texas, Stewart Field, New York, and Hendricks Army Air Field, Florida, and then broke into the jet flying business at Nellis Air Force Base, Nevada.

World War II ended before Broughton could participate in combat missions, but Korea was a different story. There he flew Lockheed F-80C Shooting Stars with the 8th Fighter-Bomber Squadron, 49th Fighter-Bomber Group, stationed at Taegu Air Base. "We could not go as high as the MiGs and we could not go as fast as the MiGs," Broughton recalled. "Our prime mission was supporting our ground forces." When forced to, however, he wasn't afraid to tangle with the MiGs, as he did the day he and his wingman encountered 16 MiGs, eventually somehow driving them off.

Broughton's squadron was also used to destroy ground supplies and materiel, most notable of which was a dawn flight in which he and his wingmen caught five trains out in the open before they could find refuge in tunnels until nighttime, when they could be moved without being seen. Between them, the F-80Cs "zinged" four of the locomotives, while the fifth one, making for the tunnel as fast it could go, ended up slamming into one that had already been hit. "He blew pretty good," Broughton said in his interview with *Veterans Chronicles*. "Then we headed up into the weather and got home to our base before breakfast with five locomotives and trains under our belt."

After Korea, Broughton commanded the renowned Air Force Thunderbirds for three years, as the group transitioned from straight-wing F-84s to swept-wing F-84s to F-100C supersonic aircraft, the first aerobatic team to do so.

As the hydraulic pressure in Broughton's F-105 dropped, so did the altitude of his aircraft. Slowly and gently, he pulled it up from its dive, which had reached almost treetop level, and managed to skillfully nudge the plane to 23,000 feet, all the while working to extinguish the fire, which he was finally able to do. Limping along, with the hydraulic pressure periodically falling to zero, he caught sight of an emergency landing strip where he was able to safely put the aircraft down.

Colonel Jacksel M. Broughton

Broughton retired from the Air Force in August 1968. After the war, he worked as a pilot for Antilles Air Boats in Fajardo, Puerto Rico, Conroy Aircraft in Santa Barbara, California, and as a technical planning advisor for Rockwell International on the space shuttle *Endeavour*.

Jacksel Broughton and his wife Alice reside in Lake Forest, California.

RED TAILS OVER ITALY

ROSCOE BROWN Veteran

"The Germans knew about the black airmen. They called them the 'black angels.' They knew we were good."

Roscoe Brown, on flying against German fighters as a Tuskegee Airman, from an interview with *Veterans Chronicles*

They were almost over their target. It was March 24, 1944. Below them, the Daimler-Benz factory continued to churn out tanks in the last days of what had become a desperate war effort for Adolph Hitler's Nazi Germany. The B-17s were escorted by five fighter groups, including a squadron of "Red Tail" fighters, which had gained fame for the red-painted tails on their P-51 Mustangs. Known as the Tuskegee Airmen, they were the first African-American fighter pilots to serve in the U.S. armed forces.

The flight was so long, the Red Tails—officially the 100th Fighter Squadron of the 332nd Fighter Group—were to be relieved along the way, except that the relief fighters were delayed and failed to show up at the rendezvous point on time. With an eye on the fuel supply, the Red Tails decided that they had to continue on rather than leave the bombers without air support. By the time they returned to their home base in Ramitelli, Italy—if they made it—they would have flown 1,600 miles, a record for the 15th Air Force.

Pilots of the legendary Tuskegee Airmen, the first African-American military aviators in the U.S. armed forces.

Acting squadron commander on this mission, Roscoe Brown anxiously scanned the sky for the enemy planes, for he knew the Germans would do what they could to protect the factory… and that meant that before long, he'd be running into the Luftwaffe's most formidable weapon, the Me-262 jet aircraft. And he was right.

"Bogies, nine o'clock. Drop your tanks and follow me," he called out to the rest of the flight group.

The encounter in the skies over Berlin was the culmination of growing respect and increasing responsibility for the Tuskegee

Airmen, due to their courage and skills as aviators and their exceptional dependability in protecting Allied bomber fleets. Bomber crews began to call them "Red-Tail Angels" because they stayed so close to the bombers, and often asked for them to be the fighter escort on their missions.

As tough as the Germans were, the larger fight for the Tuskegee Airmen was racial discrimination, for the U.S. military at the beginning of the war was still segregated. Outside the military, it was a fact of life in America that Brown had experienced daily, having grown up in all-black schools. "When you're young, you hope you can do something about it, but you can't."

Segregated restaurants, separate sections in theaters, the back of buses, public fountains that were for whites only… such was the law of the land in the 1920s and '30s.

After graduating from Dunbar High School in Washington, DC, Brown got his first taste of being treated for *who* he was, not *what* he was, by attending Springfield College in Springfield, Massachusetts, which was an integrated college… 16 blacks out of about 650 students. Brown was valedictorian of his class. Having a long-term interest in aviation stoked by the exploits of Charles Lindbergh and the air racers and barnstormers of the 1930s, Brown jumped at the chance to sign up as a Tuskegee Airman when recruited on the Springfield campus in his junior year.

The Tuskegee Airmen was an experiment to train blacks as pilots and navigators, the military building the Tuskegee Army Airfield for that purpose in Tuskegee, Alabama, where Brown learned to fly P-40 fighters. After basic training, he moved on to combat training—dogfighting—in Walterboro, South Carolina, and by August 1944, found himself in Europe flying combat missions. "The Tuskegee Airmen, because of our excellence, debunked the myths that blacks couldn't do certain things."

He needed all his training and skills that March 25th day when confronting the Me-262, the most advanced aircraft the Germans had. Following a combat maneuver he had practiced, Brown performed a "split-S." Rolling his plane and dropping below the bombers, he pulled hard to the right in a half loop, came up on an Me-262, and fired two volleys with his machine guns. The plane burst into flames, the German pilot ejecting himself from the cockpit, and Brown had the first "kill" of an Me-262 by the Red Tails.

Captain Roscoe C. Brown, Jr.

For his accomplishments in combat, Brown was awarded the Distinguished Flying Cross and the Air Medal with eight Oak Leaf Clusters. The 332nd Fighter Group—which downed three Me-262 planes that day—received the Presidential Unit Citation for the mission, the highest honor bestowed upon a combat unit.

Roscoe Brown flew a total of 68 combat missions as a Tuskegee Airman, leaving military service in 1945 with the rank of captain. After the war, he got his Ph.D. from New York University, where he became a professor, and later was president of Bronx Community College. Active in numerous organizations, he lives in Riverdale, New York.

LAST AMERICAN TO SERVE IN WORLD WAR I

FRANK BUCKLES Veteran

"I'd been advised by one of the older sergeants that a way to get to France quickly was to go into the ambulance corps, because the French were begging for ambulance service."

Frank Buckles, on joining up to fight in World War I, from an interview with *Veterans Chronicles*

When Frank Buckles was born in 1901, William McKinley was president of the United States. At the time Buckles died in 2011, he was the last surviving American veteran of World War I. In between was a remarkable life of patriotism and service to his country.

As the war raged in Europe, 13-year-old Buckles followed what was happening overseas by avidly reading about the German invasion of Belgium and France in the local newspapers as the armies settled into entrenched positions and attempted to outflank each other, with casualties building up on both sides. As Buckles stated, "Papers were all full of events of the war."

After the sinking of seven U.S. merchant ships by German submarines, America entered the war in April 1917 and was soon sending thousands of soldiers to France. Anxious to do his part, Buckles sought to enlist in the Marines, and though he was only 16 at the time, he claimed to be 18.

It didn't work. He was rejected for being too small. So it was on to the Navy, but he was again rejected, this time for having flat feet. Suspecting that it was really because he looked too young to be 18, he decided on another tack: he would try the Army next and pretend that he was 21. Somehow it worked, and he was able to enlist.

In signing up, one of the sergeants suggested that he should have a middle initial to help identify him, so he became "Frank Woodruff Buckles," the same name as that of his uncle. Another sergeant indicated that if he wanted to get to France and into the war quickly, he should sign up for the ambulance corps, because the French desperately needed ambulance drivers.

The last living American to serve in World War I, Frank W. Buckles, is honored by the U.S. Army in the American Veterans Center's National Memorial Day Parade on Constitution Avenue in Washington, DC.

Buckles was sent to boot camp at Fort Logan, Colorado, and then received intensive training in trench warfare at Fort Riley, Kansas. He sailed for England in December 1917 on the *Carpathia*, the same ship that rescued the survivors of the *Titanic* five years earlier. "We were welcomed in Britain. We were welcomed in France." After three and a half years of war, living and dying in dirt trenches, the Brits and French soldiers were tired of war and happy for the help of the "doughboys."

For the next several months, Private Buckles drove ambulances and motorcycles for the Army's 1st Fort Riley Casual Detachment. He would later comment that there was never a lack of blown-up bodies that needed to be rushed to the nearest medical unit. Finally, with America in the war, at the 11th hour on the 11th day of the 11th month in 1918, the guns fell silent. The Armistice was in effect. "I didn't find that people were so jubilant," Buckles recalled in his interview with *Veterans Chronicles*. "It was more of a relief to them the war had ended."

Buckles' immediate assignment after the war was to escort former prisoners of war back to Germany. He was promoted to corporal on September 22, 1919, and received an honorable discharge from the service in November 1919.

Buckles then attended a business school in Oklahoma City, Oklahoma, and subsequently worked at a shipping company in Toronto, Canada. In the early 1920s, he served with the 7th Regiment of the New York National Guard in New York City. By the late 1930s, he worked for the White Star and W. R. Grace steamship companies, and with the rerouting of shipping lanes to the Far East as German armies steamrolled through Europe, Buckles found himself in the Philippines, where he remained for a time, helping to resupply U.S. troops.

Then, the Japanese attacked Pearl Harbor, and Buckles, living on Manila, was soon captured. For the next three years and two months, he was a civilian internee in the Santo and Los Baños prison camps, where he existed on a starvation diet of mush. "I was one of the few who survived." And he did so through a determination to live and by "keeping myself in as good a shape as possible, as much as possible."

Despite his efforts, which included leading his fellow prisoners in calisthenics, he developed beriberi and his weight dropped below 100 pounds. He was allowed, however, to grow a small garden, which he used to help feed the children imprisoned there.

Corporal Frank W. Buckles

Buckles was liberated by an American airborne unit in February 1945. After the war, he moved to San Francisco, California, where he got married and lived for a time. Several years later, he and his wife Audrey bought a 330-acre farm near Charles Town, West Virginia, where they raised cattle. Audrey died in 1999.

Frank Buckles passed away on February 27, 2011, at age 110. Buckles was still driving a tractor at 103 and had continued to work the farm until 105.

THE NEW ENEMY: RUSSIAN COSSACKS ON HORSEBACK

DONALD BURGETT Veteran

"If you squat down and look up into the sky, you can see something, and we saw a church steeple. We know all the paratroopers would gravitate toward that church steeple, for that was the center of town."

Don Burgett, on parachuting over Normandy during the early morning hours of D-Day, from an interview with *Veterans Chronicles*

The night sky was filled with flak, as the C-47s, transporting men of the 101st Airborne, crossed the English Channel into Normandy. It was the early morning of June 6, 1944. Enveloped by a rain cloud, the planes, which had been flying so close together they had to keep their wing lights on, soon began to fall out of formation. As Private Donald Burgett's plane came out on the other side of the cloud, it was pitch black below, no signals from the Pathfinders—the planes were now beyond their drop zones—no lights burning in the villages.* Into the blackness, Burgett and the rest of the stick in his C-47 jumped, not knowing what was beneath them.

Waves and waves of paratroopers drop into Holland during Operation Market Garden, the unsuccessful Allied attempt to secure a pathway into Germany and end the war before Christmas, 1944.

Fortunately, he landed in a field, though as he later discovered, he was 12 miles from his drop zone. Soon he was joined by three others of the 101st, and suddenly, they found themselves under heavy enemy fire. "The Germans were opening up on us," Burgett recalled. "There were a lot of fireworks... mortar shells... machine guns cross-firing." The men dropped into a ditch, and then in the darkness, moved off before the Germans could zero in on their position with their 81mm mortars.

As dawn approached, they were joined by others from both the 82nd and the 101st, and the men began to head toward a church steeple, which they could barely make out in the sky that was gradually growing lighter. There they knew most of the paratroopers would gather.

* The Pathfinders dropped into Normandy about an hour before the main body of paratroopers to set up signaling devices that would transmit drop zone locations to the lead planes.

In the days that followed, the fighting was constant, as the Germans were entrenched and hidden behind tall hedges, called hedgerows, that bordered the fields throughout Normandy. Taking out the artillery emplacements and machine gun nests was slow and costly, as the German Wehrmacht and the Waffen-SS hotly contested the inland advance of the Allies. According to Burgett, the Germans began to call the men of the 101st "the butchers with the big pockets," a reference to both their fighting skills and their jumpsuits with oversized pockets.

The fiercest opposition, however, came from the Russian Cossacks on horseback.

Born in Detroit, Michigan, and raised during the Depression, Burgett probably never heard of the Cossacks much before he saw one coming at him through a hedgerow in Normandy. He was only 16 when America entered the war after Pearl Harbor. On his 18th birthday, he joined the Army and, having received basic training at Fort Riley, Kansas, with the last active horse cavalry unit in the U.S., he was able to transfer to the Army paratroops at Fort Benning, Georgia. After completing paratrooper training, he joined the 101st Airborne Division in England, where he was assigned to the 506th Parachute Infantry Regiment.

He wasn't long in Normandy before he had his first encounter with the Cossacks. "They would come down through the hedgerows, guiding their horses with their knees, a gun in one hand and a saber in the other. We shot a lot of them out of their saddles. They'd cut you in half with that saber, if they got a good swing at you."

After Normandy, Burgett and the men in his regiment were sent back to England for a short rest and to reequip and replace the dead and wounded they had lost in Normandy. Not long after, Burgett was jumping into Holland as part of Operation Market Garden, an unsuccessful Allied mission in September 1944 to capture bridges across the Maas and Rhine rivers before the Germans could blow them up.

A month later, the 101st was headed to support the 28th Infantry, trying desperately to fend off the German army encircling the town of Bastogne, Belgium, as Hitler began the Battle of the Bulge by throwing 55 divisions against the Allies in a surprise attack through the Ardennes. The bitter cold combined with the lack of food, warm clothing, ammunition, and even medical supplies, along with waist-high snow in places, made for some of the toughest fighting conditions of the war. Finally, on December 26th, General George C. Patton's Third Army was able to punch through the German lines and the siege was lifted.

Private Donald R. Burgett

For Burgett, the war was not quite over, as he fought with the 506th all the way to Hitler's home in Austria. He was discharged on December 31, 1945. Afterward, he worked as a carpenter and a residential homebuilder, and later he became an author of four books.

Donald Burgett resides with his wife Twyla in Howell, Michigan.

THE TAKING OF HILL 362

FRANK CALDWELL Veteran

"All my officers were killed. I managed to lead this company through some terrible fortifications, and we captured more territory than any other outfit… and we took more casualties."

Frank Caldwell, on the action of Fox Company in capturing Hill 362 on Iwo Jima, from an interview with *Veterans Chronicles*

The Japanese had been driven from the south end of the island, and the American flag flew over Mount Suribachi. The north end of Iwo Jima, however, remained firmly in enemy hands. The rocky terrain was riddled with caves and bunkers in which the Japanese would burrow themselves, relatively safe from American artillery and the bombardment which usually preceded an advancement by the 5th Marine Division.

Perhaps the most iconic photo of World War II, the Stars and Stripes is raised upon Mount Suribachi on Iwo Jima. Joe Rosenthal's legendary photo is actually of the second flag to be raised on the mountain, erected to replace a smaller flag that had been raised a short time earlier.

March 3, 1945. Frank Caldwell, captain of the 2nd Battalion of Fox Company in the 26th Marine Regiment, had been on the island for 13 days, and of the 258 men he brought ashore with him on February 19th, he was down considerably in numbers. The battalion had run into a pocket of resistance a few days prior, as it slowly made its way from cave to cave toward the upper end of the island. On one day alone, eliminating the Japanese machine gun nests and mortars had resulted in 59 casualties. According to Caldwell, "The Japanese were well dug in. They had excellent bunkers."

For the 5th Division, the task ahead was certain to be costly, for the Japanese still had the equivalent of eight infantry divisions on the island and a tank regiment, plus two artillery and three heavy mortar battalions. With tunnels connecting the gun emplacements, the enemy was going to be difficult to dig out.

For Caldwell personally, the situation was particularly difficult, for he had no officers. They had all been killed. Other than a few NCOs (non-commission officers… sergeants), he was alone in leading his men.

Caldwell was born and raised in Spartanburg, South Carolina. He went to Davidson College in North Carolina, got an Army commission through the ROTC program, and was able to switch to the Marine Corps. While at Quantico, Virginia, he decided he wanted to be a parachutist, and got airborne training at Camp Lejune, North Carolina, where he received his wings. He was assigned to the 1st Marine Parachute Division and sent to New Caledonia in the Pacific as a platoon leader, executive officer, and commander of A Company, Parachute Battalion. He was in combat against the Japanese in the Solomon Islands on Guadalcanal, Vella Lavella, and Bougainville.

In February 1944, the parachute units were deactivated, and Caldwell was sent back to the states to Camp Pendleton, California, where he joined the 5th Marine Division, 3rd Battalion, 26th Marine Regiment as executive officer. Within a month, he was promoted to captain and became commander of Fox Company, 2nd Battalion. From Pendleton, the division was sent to Hawaii, where they trained further for a number of months, not knowing where they were going next. It turned out to be Iwo Jima. In less than three weeks, he was on the island, and 12 days later, he was leading his men against some of the most difficult fortifications on the island.

"We had several flame-throwers, recoilless rifles, explosives, and we had three rifle platoons of 39 Marines each, divided up into squads and fire teams. We had a number of water-cooled Browning machine guns and A-4 machine guns. We had one BAR* in each fire team." Of all the weapons, the flame-throwers and grenades were undoubtedly the most useful in eliminating the Japanese taking refuge in the caves.

The toughest fight, according to Caldwell, was in capturing Hill 362, as the units were raked by machine guns on the flanks. A number of tanks either became the target of interlocking fire, or were blown up by buried land mines. "I got hit in the thigh with shrapnel from a bursting artillery round," Caldwell said in his interview with *Veterans Chronicles*. "I turned myself into sickbay. They patched me up, and I went back in." There was little time for rest. "Moving back 20 yards and hiding behind a boulder was rest to us."

* BAR = Browning Automatic Rifle

Colonel Frank C. Caldwell

Finally, on March 16th, Iwo Jima was declared secured, though limited fighting went on with remnants of the Japanese army. Days later, Caldwell and his men boarded ship and returned to Hawaii. Of the 258 men who had landed with him on Iwo Jima, only 20 were left, the others either having been killed in battle or wounded and evacuated. Fox Company had captured more territory than any other outfit on Iwo Jima.

Caldwell later served in Korea as executive officer for the 2nd Battalion, 7th Marines, became an instructor at Quantico, and then was director of Marine Corps History at Headquarters Marine Corps next to Arlington Cemetery before retiring as a colonel from the service.

Frank Caldwell and his wife Peggy reside in Newport, Rhode Island.

TWENTY MILES AND TEN DAYS TO BASTOGNE

ROBERT CALVERT, JR. Veteran

"We had three different platoon sergeants in the course of five or six days. At one time, our company had zero officers in it. The first two were hit in an ambush. My platoon leader was hit sleeping at night."

Bob Calvert, on the drive to reach Bastogne, France, during the Battle of the Bulge, from an interview with *Veterans Chronicles*

The tanks, half-tracks, and armored vehicles of the 4th Division crawled out of the woods. On the other side of the open field, men in foxholes were peering over their carbines at them, unsure who they were facing. The lieutenant yelled across, "This is the 4th Armored." Moments later, the answer came back, "101st Airborne. Glad to see you."

Bastogne, Belgium, had finally been reached. It had taken ten days to go 20 miles, days of intense fighting as they forged their way over roads covered with ice, and in places, deep snow. Hitler's final campaign to destroy the Allied armies, later known as the Battle of the Bulge, was underway, and Bastogne was the middle of the German offensive.

Soldiers walk through the bombed-out town of Bastogne during the Battle of the Bulge, Christmas Day, 1944.

Private Robert Calvert of the 51st Armored Infantry Battalion, C Company recalled the moment he looked across the field. "I went up to make personal contact, say 'hello.' They were a very heroic outfit." Bastogne had been completely surrounded by elements of the German XLVII Panzer Corps, and inside the defensive perimeter of the 101st, men were starving and freezing and were almost out of ammunition. If the siege had gone on much longer, the Germans would have been able to walk into Bastogne. Fortunately, as the skies cleared, some relief had come a few days prior with the dropping of food and ammunition from C-47s circling above.

And then, the 4th showed up, breaking the enemy stranglehold on the village. Behind the tanks, 200 trucks with supplies and ambulances for evacuating the wounded rolled into Bastogne.

For Calvert, the 20 miles to Bastogne in the frigid, sub-zero weather and blowing snow was an ordeal he never forgot. Any illusions he might have had about the "glories of war" were long gone. Calvert was born in California, but raised in Scarsdale, New York. When Pearl Harbor happened, he was only 18, so he knew he could probably spend another year at Oberlin College. He entered the Army in May 1943, was sent first to Camp Upton in New York, and was then was put on a train for Macon, Georgia, where he underwent basic training at Camp Wheeler for a total of 17 weeks.

Calvert was in a special program called the Army Specialized Training Program, or ASTP, which didn't last all that long, for Army Chief of Staff General George C. Marshall needed more men sooner than ASTP would give him, and rather than draft fathers, the decision was made to dump the 140,000 men in ASTP back into the ranks. In time, after training at Fort Leonard Wood, Missouri, and Camp Reynolds in Pennsylvania, Calvert finally ended up at Camp Shanks, New York, where, in June 1944, he embarked for Liverpool, England.

In England, he languished for a time before being sent in September 1944 to Normandy. The war had moved inland by that time, but there was plenty of fighting left to do. In France, he was stationed in Etampes, not far from Paris, and then in a town a called Chalons in Vosges. Finally, the day after Thanksgiving, Calvert got his orders. He was assigned to the 4th Armored Division, 51st Armored Infantry Battalion. And then, on the 16th of December, the German army began its assault on the Allied front. Hitler's *blitzkrieg* was a complete surprise.

In thinking back to those ten days, Calvert recalled that getting to Bastogne may have seemed easy to a planner back in Third Army Headquarters looking at a map, "but the ground was covered with snow. The tankers couldn't see whether there was a ravine, or a rock." On one night in particular, "they stopped and made a circle like covered wagons would do in the old days, and we were stuck there for the night." It was so cold, by the next morning "we lost some 17 people, because of frostbite, or pneumonia, including our company commander and our platoon sergeant."

In reaching Bastogne, the 4th Armored had little time for resting, for the war went on. "There were Germans all around the place. We spent the next two weeks dug in to keep the corridor we had established open."

Calvert was made squad leader after the battle, and had ten men: three former cooks, three refugees from coastal artillery, two fathers who didn't need to be there, and two young kids just out of basic training. "Before the war was over, every single one of them was killed or wounded."

After the war, Robert Calvert went back to Oberlin College to get his degree. He worked as an administrator at four colleges, spent four years with the Peace Corps, and became a book publisher. He and his wife Janice reside in Garret Park, Maryland.

SURVIVING THE DEATH RAILWAY

H. ROBERT CHARLES Veteran

"They said that if anyone tried to escape, they would kill all of us. If you fell down, they would shoot you or just leave you."

Bob Charles, on being captured by the Japanese after the sinking of the USS *Houston*, from an interview with *Veterans Chronicles*

He could see the shore ahead of him, and after nine hours in the water, it almost didn't matter what awaited him. (He knew the time because his Elgin watch was still ticking.) Private First Class Robert Charles, a machine gunner on the now-sunk heavy cruiser USS *Houston*, had reached the Indonesian island of Java in the South Pacific, and as soon as he did, he became a captive of Japanese soldiers. "The Japs had a machine gun," Charles recalled, "and they were already pointing it at a group covered with oil with their hands up. They spoke Japanese to you, and you quickly learned Japanese after that."

"The Galloping Ghost of the Java Coast"—the USS Houston—prior to its sinking in the Battle of Sunda Strait, March 1, 1942.

Late in the day on February 28, 1942, the *Houston* and a second heavy cruiser, the USS *Perth*, had run into a Japanese battle fleet as they passed through Sunda Strait between Java and Sumatra in the Java Sea. Their means of retreat blocked by a Japanese destroyer squadron, the cruisers came under heavy fire, with the *Perth* going down in the first hour, leaving the *Houston* to fight alone against the armada of Japanese warships.

Hit by torpedoes and bursting artillery shells, the *Houston* lost headway and came to a stop as the Japanese destroyers moved in, machine-gunning the decks. Shortly afterwards, the ship rolled over and sank to the bottom. Of the 1,061 officers and men on board the *Houston*—including a detachment of 74 Marines—693 lives were lost. The remaining 368 survived long enough to become prisoners of the Japanese. Including Charles.

"They marched us on a hot asphalt road, and all of us were barefoot." Stuffed into the hold of a ship that had recently transported animals and forced to lie at night on cow dung, they eventually reached Burma and a jungle camp set up for the building of a railway using the prisoners as slave labor.* "You got up at dawn and you worked until dark. Seven days a week."

Charles, in a twist of fate, may have been better prepared for the harsh treatment by the Japanese guards than many of the men in the compound, for he had been severely and continually abused as a youth by his stepfather. "He used a blacksnake whip on me… and the beatings I took at the slightest provocation probably toughened me up," he said. "I was in excellent shape when I went in."

Charles was born in Pitcher, Oklahoma, and raised on a wheat farm in Partridge, Kansas. His memories were both of what he didn't have growing up that other kids had, and the hatred and meanness of his stepfather, both toward his family and toward his neighbors. Charles left as soon as he felt he could, and was raised by two foster families before enlisting in the Marines in June 1940. While staying with the second foster family, he finished high school and went to junior college for a year and a half, helped out by people who paid for his books and other expenses.

Charles credits the fact that he managed to survive two years as a slave laborer in the Burmese camp to fellow prisoner Henri "Doc" Hekking, a doctor with the Dutch Colonial Army. Hekking taught him the value of plants—and their components such as chlorophyll—in treating diseases. Eventually, the Japanese began to accept that the plants could keep their prisoners healthier and thus better able to work.

Hekking and Charles were allowed to search for the herbs in the surrounding jungle, accompanied by two or three guards. Scratches on arms and legs were a common occurrence, and untreated, they would likely turn into an ulcer that could eat straight to the bone. Treated by Hekking, ulcers were never a problem, and gradually, skeptics became believers. As Charles reported in an interview with *Veterans Chronicles*, "He used his knowledge of the jungle to help save lives."

After the work was finished on the railway, Charles and other prisoners were taken to Saigon, Vietnam, where they remained until liberated by British paratroopers and OSS (Office of Strategic Services) operatives at the end of the war. He recovered for several weeks in a hospital in Calcutta, India. Arriving back in the U.S., he was surprised to learn that the military, and the public, had no knowledge of what happened to the *Houston*. It was assumed sunk, but confirmation was possible only after the prisoners came home and told their stories of the Battle of Sunda Strait.

Following the war, Charles finished his college education and had a long career in journalism.

H. Robert Charles passed away in Rockwall, Texas, on December 3, 2009.

Private First Class H. Robert Charles

* Charles was forced to work on the infamous Burma Railway, also known as the Death Railway, ultimately linking Burma and Thailand.

CARING FOR THE SICK AND DYING AT MAUTHAUSEN

EVANGELINE COEYMAN Veteran

"One of the ladies told me they knew when the people were going to the crematory, that they shaved their hair and took the gold out of their teeth."

Evangeline Coeyman, on her assignment as an Army nurse to the liberated concentration camp of Mauthausen, from an interview with *Veterans Chronicles*

The camp had been liberated by the U.S. 11th Armored Division on May 5, 1945. Days later, Second Lieutenant Evangeline Coeyman entered through the gates of the Mauthausen Concentration Camp in Austria. The German guards had either fled or surrendered, and the 11th had started to clean the camp up, but an offensive odor still emanated from the crematory. The vast population of former prisoners—for the most part, Poles and Russians—remained, many simply lying in their bunks, awaiting their fate.

The war in Europe was over. Recognizing the desperate need for food and medications, Coeyman and a contingent of nurses formerly attached to the 59th Field Hospital of the 90th Infantry Division had been allowed into Mauthausen to care for the ill and dying. "I would say the men were harder to take care of than the women," Coeyman reported in an interview with *Veterans Chronicles*. They curled themselves almost into a fetal position. "I suppose they were hungry... and cold." They were emaciated and had what was called the thousand-yard stare. "The women socialized a little more, which I thought made the difference."

Graves of those killed in Nazi camps, stretching as far as the eyes can see.

Coeyman soon found that tuberculosis, typhoid fever, cholera, and undulant fever inflicted many in the camp, and deaths occurred daily, though by the time she got there most of "the sickest ones had already died." More deaths occurred in the early mornings than at other times, according to Coeyman, when the body metabolism is at its lowest point. Fortunately, there was always a corpsman to help, as lifting down a body from a top bunk was difficult, even in its emaciated condition. (The bunks were three high.) The corpses were placed on flat-top wagons and drawn by four to six men to a mass grave.

Particularly repugnant to Coeyman were inner barracks reportedly used for experimental surgery, especially on women. In one of them, a German doctor who was being retained there, pointed out a lampshade made from human skin. Why he was there and not locked up somewhere else was not clear to her.

Coeyman was raised in Vera Cruz, Pennsylvania, and after she graduated from Emmaus High School in 1939, she went to St. Luke's Hospital School of Nursing in Bethlehem, Pennsylvania. Four months after graduating from nursing school, she joined the Army and was sent to Camp Claiborne in Louisiana for basic training. She worked in the hospital there for more than a year, and then was sent to Fitzsimmons General Hospital at Fort Leonard Wood in Missouri, which was "one of the big Army hospitals in the country." Her final destination in the U.S. was Fort Carson in Colorado. "We knew at that point we were going to a field hospital because we had to sleep out in a tent."

She was right. On the 6th she arrived in England, but the ship put back to sea, for it was D-Day and the English Channel had to be cleared. The *Louis Pasteur* finally docked on the 8th.

Six to eight weeks later, Coeyman was in Normandy, assigned to the 59th Field Hospital with the 90th Infantry Division. The 59th included an eight-person surgical team, four to six doctors, 18 nurses, and 50 to 70 corpsmen.

"Wherever the division moved, we moved," which meant the push through northern France, the Battle of the Bulge, the invasion of the Rhineland, and the liberation of the Flossenbürg Concentration Camp in Bavaria, Germany. "After October," she recalled, "we really started getting busy. One time before the Battle of the Bulge, we were two miles in back of the Germans." Coeyman added, "Sometimes we had to service two divisions and more than two surgical units." (In addition to the 90th, the field hospital also supported the 82nd Airborne Division during the battle, since it had no medical unit.)

Particularly severe were the cold, freezing rain, ice, and snow at Bastogne. "We were sleeping in tents, in our fatigues. We each had a duffle bag and a blanket" and slept on cots. There was a little heater in the center of the tent that helped some to take the chill off.

Second Lieutenant Evangeline R. Coeyman

From Bastogne, the 90th thrust into the heartland of Germany, and after the surrender, Coeyman was assigned to the liberated concentration camps of Mauthausen and Gosen. (She spent most of her time at Mauthausen.) Weeks later, she returned to the U.S. and went to work as a nurse for St. Luke's Hospital, where she became head nurse in 1952. She later joined the faculty of the hospital's nursing school, from which she retired in 1989.

Evangeline Coeyman lived for many years in Allentown, Pennsylvania, and today resides in Littleton, Colorado.

23

FLYING WITH THE "TORRID TURTLES"

GERALD COLEMAN Veteran

"My roommate blew up in front of me. That was the worst part of either war… to look at a woman with five kids and tell her her husband is dead."

Jerry Coleman, on the death of his best friend and roommate during a mission, from an interview with *Veterans Chronicles*

The decision was to bypass Rabaul. There would be no offensive by Allied land troops. Yet, it couldn't be ignored. Located on the island of New Britain off the coast of New Guinea, it had been the main naval base for the Japanese invasion of the Solomon Islands. In the spring of 1944, the stronghold was still formidable with some 100,000 enemy soldiers, 367 anti-aircraft guns, and five airfields.

Reducing it and destroying its defenses became the job of the Allied air forces, which included Marine Torpedo Bombing Squadron 341, known as "The Torrid Turtles." Fresh from flying air support for the retaking of Guadalcanal in VMSB-341, Second Lieutenant Jerry Coleman had been assigned in September 1944 to a strip of land 40 miles north of Bougainville in the Solomons. Green Island wasn't much wider than its two airstrips, but it was 117 miles west of Rabaul, well within the range of the Douglas SBD Dauntless dive bombers being flown by the squadron.

Baseball Heroes of World War II, Lou Brissie, Yogi Berra, Jerry Coleman, and John Miles, share their wartime experiences at an event hosted by the American Veterans Center and World War II Veterans Committee in 2010.

"The Dauntless was a dive bomber with a two-man crew," recalled Coleman. "My crewmate was Irish and was called 'Stretch.' I think I nearly frightened him to death with my flying." Stretch was the backseat gunner and radio operator. The plane was equipped with two 50-caliber machine guns, one in each wing. It also carried a single 1,000-pound bomb or two 500-pound bombs. Coleman would approach Rabaul at 12,000 feet, drop to 10,000, and begin his harrowing dive through enemy flak, picking up speed on the way down and ending as low as 1,000 feet before dropping a bomb on a gun emplacement or other target.

Coleman's interest in flying can be attributed to a visit to his high school in San Jose, California, by a couple of naval aviators. He was only 17 at the time, so he couldn't join the service until after his birthday in September 1942. "I wanted to be Joe Foss, Jr.," Coleman once said in an interview. Foss was one of the first aces in World War II, shooting down 26 Japanese planes in 44 days.

Within weeks after he reached 18, Coleman was a naval aviation cadet in the Navy's V-5 program, which was training and pumping out young flying officers for both the U.S. Navy and the Marine Corps. Over the next year and a half, he received training at bases in California, Colorado, North Carolina, and finally, Texas, where he received his wings and was commissioned a second lieutenant.

But he wasn't done. He was then trained on flying the Douglas Dauntless dive bombers at Jacksonville Naval Air Station in Jacksonville, Florida, and then, after short duty at Cherry Point, North Carolina, and El Toro, California, he was on his way to Guadalcanal as a replacement pilot. Next up, once the island was secure, was Green Island… and Rabaul.

The flight echelon of Coleman's squadron remained on Green Island until January 22, 1945, and after island hopping, soon found itself supporting ground troops during General Douglas MacArthur's return to the Philippines. In July 1945, VMSB-341 was called back to form carrier-based squadrons in preparation for an amphibious assault on Japan. Before that could happen, the U.S. dropped the atomic bombs on Hiroshima and Nagasaki, and the war was over. Coleman had flown 57 missions, and perhaps thought his career in the military was over.

But it wasn't. At the outbreak of the Korean War, he was recalled to active duty, and assigned to VMF-323, known as the "Death Rattlers." It was during a mission that his roommate and close friend was shot down in front of him. After Korea was over, Coleman was asked by the wife of his friend if her husband was really dead, as she wasn't going to believe anyone but Coleman. She had been holding out hope he had been captured. "I had to look at this woman with five kids—it bothers me to this day—the look on her face when I said, 'Yes, he died.'"

Coleman flew another 63 combat missions in Korea, flying F4U and AU-1 Corsairs.

His baseball career with the New York Yankees is well documented. In 1949, he was Rookie of Year. The following season, he was an American League All-Star and the Most Valuable Player in the World Series. He is considered to have been one of the best defensive second basemen of all time, and has been inducted into the Baseball Hall of Fame in Cooperstown, New York.

Lieutenant Colonel Gerald F. Coleman

After retiring from baseball, he became a sports announcer with the New York Yankees and later with the California Angels.

Jerry Coleman and his wife Mary reside in Santa Rosa, California.

SPIKING THE GUNS AT BRÉCOURT MANOR

LYNN COMPTON Veteran

"When I landed in Normandy, I didn't have a weapon. I didn't have any personal belongings. I didn't have any food. I had nothing but a trench knife on my belt."

Buck Compton, on the loss of his "leg bag" during his parachute jump into Normandy, from an interview with *Veterans Chronicles*

The rope broke and his leg bag dropped into the night. Jumping behind the lines into Normandy, Lieutenant Lynn "Buck" Compton had no weapons or ammunition or his medical kit, or even a toothbrush. They were all in the bag.

After landing safely in a field of cows, he collected his thoughts. Nearby, another soldier floated down in the predawn darkness, but it was no one he knew. Evidently, the planes had missed their drop points, and his division, as well as the other divisions parachuting into German-occupied France that night, were spread over the countryside. Finding the rest of the men in his platoon might be impossible. He and the other soldier could only head east toward the beach, where they knew the invasion would begin.

Along the way, they began to pick up other men. What he needed most was another gun. Finally, he came across a soldier with a badly broken leg who insisted that Compton take his gun. Should the Germans find him before the medics, he might not be shot if they saw he was unarmed. In either case, he wouldn't need a weapon.

Paratroopers prepare to board their plane for the invasion of Normandy and the Allied return to France, June 1944.

As the sky became lighter and the group neared the beach area, the booming of the Allied ships at sea was matched by the German artillery pouring heavy fire down on Utah Beach. The landing had begun. Walking along, Compton finally met up with some familiar faces, and before long, the 1st and 2nd platoons of Easy Company comprised about a dozen men. At the time, no one knew where their company commander was (his plane had been shot down), so Lieutenant Richard Winters took over as the senior officer.

As they stood and looked around the corner of a building in the farm area of Brécourt Manor, Winters and Compton both agreed that the

German 105mm howitzers firing had to be taken out. They pretty much knew where they were, and under a covering of machine gun fire, Compton crawled across a field and through a hedgerow, where he found a maze of trenches. At the end of one of the trenches, two Germans were operating one of the guns.

Confronting the Germans with his Thompson submachine gun at hip level, Compton attempted to take them out. Without hesitation he pulled the trigger, but heard only a soft *plunk*. The gun he had been given had a broken firing pin, and he faced the fully armed German soldiers with only a knife and a couple of grenades he'd never be able to get to in time.

Growing up in Los Angeles, Compton had given little thought to serving in the military until he went to UCLA. In high school and in college, he was a sports star in both football and baseball. At UCLA, though, every male student had to take two years of ROTC, and if you took another two years, you got a commission, except that Pearl Harbor came along before Compton had a chance to meet the required three months of active duty. So, he had to go through Officers Training School (OTS) before getting his commission.

After a short stint in the 176th Infantry, Compton volunteered for the parachute troops and ended up in the famed Easy Company, 2nd Battalion, 506th Parachute Infantry Regiment (PIR), 101st Airborne, and on the night of December 5, 1944, found himself in a C-47 bound for Normandy.

As he faced the Germans, convinced he was done for, he heard bursts from a submachine gun behind him. He had been followed by one of his men, who fired at one of the Germans. As the other raced across the open field, Compton threw a perfectly aimed grenade, which exploded just above the German's head, killing him instantly.

With a squad led by Compton pitching grenades into the trenches from the left and a second squad taking the right, and with other soldiers of Easy Company laying a spread of machine gun fire, the four 105mm howitzers were taken and spiked with TNT. This action is said to have saved thousands of lives on Utah Beach. In recognition of his bravery and his part in disabling the guns, Compton was awarded the Silver Star.

After returning home, Compton got his law degree from Loyola Law School in Los Angeles and was a

First Lieutenant Lynn D. Compton

detective in the Los Angeles Police Department before leaving for the district attorney's office. In 1970, governor of California Ronald Reagan appointed him associate justice of the 2nd District Court of Appeals. He retired from the bench in 1990.

Buck Compton passed away on February 25, 2012, in Burlington, Washington, his wife Donna having died in 1994.

THE ENEMY WITHIN AT CAMP NAM DONG

ROGER DONLON Veteran

"They hit us hard. They penetrated the outer perimeter, inner perimeter. Of the 300 locals we were training, 100 were VC sympathizers, and when the attack started, they turned on us immediately."

Roger Donlon, on his Special Forces team being attacked at Camp Nam Dong and the betrayal of local mercenaries, from an interview with *Veterans Chronicles*

Early morning, July 6, 1964. In the days before, the villagers had seemed nervous and scared. Captain Roger Donlon of the U.S. Army 7th Special Forces Group, Detachment A-726, knew something was about to happen, and he warned his men, "Get everyone buttoned up tight tonight, the VC [Viet Cong] are coming." What he didn't know was that Camp Nam Dong was surrounded, and of the 300 locals being trained by Donlon and his men, 100 were VC sympathizers and about to turn on them.

Donlon also had a Vietnamese counterpart who turned out to be a traitor. "He had a Hawaiian shirt on," Donlon recalled. "That was his safety tag."

The 12 Special Forces men in his detachment and the 60 Chinese mercenaries he was fortunate to have with him were about to face some 800 to 900 of the enemy. Donlon had placed four of the mercenaries in each of the five mortar pits and alerted them to what he was sure was coming.

At 2:26, it happened. Donlon had completed his rounds of the perimeter that comprised the camp, and all seemed quiet. He had just stepped through the door of the mess hall to check the guard roster, when suddenly, a mortar erupted on the building and blew him back out the door. A second round hit the command post. Quickly regaining his senses, Donlon mowed down three of the VC who had reached the main gate and then raced through a barrage of shells, grenades, and heavy gunfire for one of the mortar pits. He almost didn't make it, for he was tossed into the air by an exploding shell that wounded him in the stomach.

Roger Donlon is awarded the Medal of Honor by President Lyndon B. Johnson. Donlon was the first man to be awarded the military's highest honor for valor in Vietnam.

Fighting dizziness, he crawled into the pit, where he found that most of the men there had been wounded.

For Donlon, being in the service was inevitable. Born and raised in Saugerties, New York, he was the eighth child in a family of ten children. His father had fought in World War I and all four of his brothers (a sister and another brother had died) ended up in the military. After attending a Catholic school for eight years, he then went to Saugerties High School. Eventually he decided that he wanted to go to flight school, and in particular, the recently founded Air Force Academy. Unfortunately, he was rejected by an eye doctor who discovered a congenital cataract in his left eye.

After following a path that included a year at West Point, getting married, and moving to Louisiana, Donlon decided to enlist in the Army and was sent to Fort Chafee, Arkansas, and from there to Officer Candidate School (OCS). "I reset my compass," he said in the interview with *Veterans Chronicles*.

Further training included U.S. Army Special Warfare School at Fort Bragg, California. After a stint on skis in Alaska and nine weeks at Fort Greely, Donlon left the snow and cold of the 49th state and was assigned as a Green Beret to Detachment A-726, headed for Vietnam, and soon after, Camp Nam Dong.

Directing the movement of the wounded men to safety, Donlon remained behind in the gunpit covering their withdrawal. Upon noticing that his sergeant was injured in a nearby hole and unable to evacuate, Donlon crawled over to him. In attempting to pull him out, another mortar exploded close by, spraying shrapnel into Donlon's shoulder.

For five hours, Donlon moved from position to position, dragging ammo and supplies to where they were needed, directing the mortar and machine gun fire on the VC, moving wounded men to cover, tearing his shirt into bandages, and all the time, fending off the enemy with covering fire.

When dawn finally broke and the VC drifted back into the jungle, Marine choppers appeared above the camp. Nam Dong had held. Of the Americans, Sergeant John Houston had died and most of the other 11 were wounded. Of the South Vietnamese who had remained loyal, 55 had died and 65 were wounded. Exposed as he was to enemy fire, Donlon had been wounded seven times during the night, with shrapnel in the face, arms, feet, and stomach.

Colonel Roger H. C. Donlon

Donlon's team would be one of the most highly decorated units in Army history.

In March 1967, Donlon was appointed to major and assigned to the 2nd Infantry Division in South Korea, where he commanded the Advanced Combat Training Academy. He returned to South Vietnam for a second tour in January 1972 as a district senior advisor in Kien Hoa Province.

After retiring from the service, he has remained active in representing the Special Forces Regiment as an advisor and mentor. He is also an active director of the Westmoreland Scholarship Foundation.

Colonel Roger Donlon and his wife Norma reside in Leavenworth, Kansas.

UNDER THE MICROSCOPE ON "ELEANOR'S FOLLY"

LORENZO DUFAU Veteran

"This is something I wanted to do. I would feel better, opening doors for my son and others. I wanted to prove that we were as much American as anybody."

Lorenzo DuFau, on his service with the historic USS *Mason*, one of the first ships to integrate in the U.S. Navy, from an interview with *Veterans Chronicles*

The ship was called the USS *Mason*. Probably, Signalman Third Class Lorenzo DuFau had no idea that it was to become the role model for integration of the U.S. Navy. All he knew was that he was going to sea with an all-black crew, one of 150 men to step aboard ship on a March day in 1944 that was so cold, there was ice in Boston harbor, where it had just been commissioned.* Worse, the *Mason* itself had no heat.

* A second ship with an all-black crew, the USS *PC-1264*, was classified as a submarine chaser, and it was commissioned a month after the USS *Mason*. It was used for coastal convoy and anti-submarine duty along the Atlantic seaboard.

The crew of the USS *Mason* on deck while anchored at New York Harbor, 1944.

The USS *Mason* was an experiment, black crews and white officers, though at the beginning of World War II, General Dwight D. Eisenhower had integrated troops on the battlefield to solve a desperate need early on for manpower. Doing so took on two problems: the culture of racial segregation that permeated both the military and civilian life in America, and the myth that black men simply could not fight as well and be depended on like white men. They were typically relegated to mundane tasks.

As DuFau recalled after he heard about Pearl Harbor, "I wondered what I could do to help defend my country. With all the warts and rocks, America was still home to me."

Black men serving with distinction in the trenches and in the skies as bomber and fighter pilots began to dispel the notion about their bravery, their abilities in action, and their commitment to winning the war. Then there was the USS *Mason*, a destroyer escort charged with the responsibility of protecting convoys crossing the Atlantic from enemy submarines and surface ships. As the *Mason* left Boston Harbor for a shakedown cruise in the warmer waters of Bermuda, the men on board wondered how they were going to be received in the ports of England and Ireland, where they would soon be headed.

Raised in New Orleans, Louisiana, DuFau was married at 19. Six months after hearing about Pearl Harbor, though he had two children by then, he knew he had to do something, so in June 1942, he enlisted in the Navy. The officer who signed him up told him, "You don't need to go in the service. You're 3A." But he felt he had to, not only because he wanted to fight for his country, but also because "I wanted to be part of the integration movement. I wanted to prove that we were as much American as anybody."

In June, he was sent to boot camp at Great Lakes, Illinois, where he went to signalman's school and became a Signalman Third Class. After nine months aboard a Coast Guard vessel, he was sent to Virginia for destroyer escort training, including sending and receiving Morse Code with flags and blinking lights.

Not long after, he was assigned to the USS *Mason*, conveying ships loaded with supplies and men across the Atlantic. His first convoy docked in Belfast, Ireland, for refueling and food, and it was there they learned how they would be received abroad, for they were greeted warmly by the people, one lady apologizing "because the sun wasn't shining." They had stout in a local pub, where "the old-timers put us to shame."

On October 18, 1944, during a convoy, the ships in the convoy were hit hard by a North Atlantic storm so severe it split the deck of the *Mason*. The men not only self-repaired the critical structural damage, they also rescued other ships in the convoy, an action for which the crew received a letter of commendation for meritorious service.

During its six convoys, including three trips to North Africa, "we knew we were under the microscope." The *Mason*, in fact, was called "Eleanor's Folly," a reference to Eleanor Roosevelt, wife of President Franklin D. Roosevelt, who ardently advocated for an end to segregation in the armed forces.

At the end of the war, DuFau was sent to Florida for a while to train young officers. The USS *Mason* was decommissioned on October

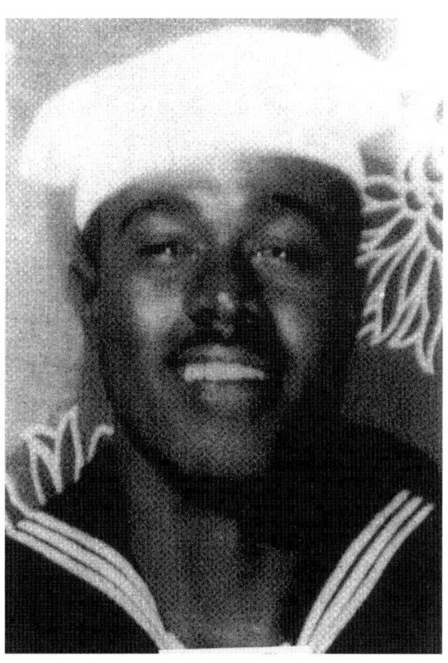

Signalman First Class Lorenzo A. DuFau

12, 1945, and sold for scrap in 1947. After returning home, DuFau was unable to find a job that matched his training, so "I pushed a cart around in the garment industry for $35 a week and drove a cab for a while." Eventually he went to work in the construction industry.

Lorenzo DuFau resides today in the Bronx in New York City.

CONFRONTING THE ENEMY AT GOVILLE

WALTER EHLERS Veteran

"I told the company commander, you better have the medics look at my back. He sees this bullet hole in my back. 'My God, you have been shot clear through. You should be dead.'"

Walter Ehlers, on his wound the day he won the Medal of Honor on Normandy, from an interview with *Veterans Chronicles*

It was three days after D-Day, June 8, 1944. Staff Sergeant Walter Ehlers and his squad had worked their way some eight miles inland from Omaha Beach and had reached the small town of Goville. He was fortunate to have gotten that far, for he had already escaped the devastating fire of German machine guns and artillery on the first day, carefully picked his way through minefields, overtook pillboxes pouring fire down on the beaches, and captured a number of the enemy along the way.

Two nights before, in chasing a German patrol that plowed through his camp, Ehlers and his platoon found a briefcase dropped in the road by the fleeing patrol. Ehlers took it back to his company commander, who turned it over to battalion headquarters. Inside, it was a map of the second and third lines of defense for the retreating Germans. The platoon now had an idea where the Germans were, but rooting them out and running them down were going to be difficult.

Omaha Beach on the afternoon of D-Day, June 6, 1944. The beach is strewn with wrecked trucks, a Sherman tank, German obstructions, and American casualties.

Early morning found Ehlers and his men crossing an open field outside of Goville, when the platoon came under fire. Rushing them behind a nearby hedgerow, Ehlers moved down along the hedgerow by himself and started up another one. He could hear the machine gun somewhere up ahead, but he had no idea who and what he would be facing before he got to it. He soon found out, as he suddenly came upon four German soldiers, with their guns pointed at him.

Ehlers probably owes his being in the Army to his older brother, Roland, who in 1940 enlisted with him in the 17th Infantry Regiment of the 7th Infantry Division. A third brother, Claus, spent three years in the Pacific, fighting with General Douglas

MacArthur's 24th Infantry Division. Growing up on a farm in Kansas, the boys were close and worked hard with their parents in raising cattle and hogs and in growing vegetables, especially during the tough periods of drought and floods.

Pearl Harbor happened shortly after the boys got a weekend pass to go skiing on Mount Rainier. When the announcement came over the radio, they took off their skis and returned to their units. After amphibious training at Camp Pendleton, California, they were sent across the country to Camp Pickett, Virginia, where they got new equipment and rifles and a French translation book. But instead of going to France, they were put on a ship to Africa, where they invaded a city north of Casablanca, became part of the 1st Division, and participated in the invasion of Sicily.

Back in England, Walter and Roland were separated because of a new rule in the military due to all five of the Sullivan brothers having served on board the *Juneau*; the light cruiser was sunk by a Japanese torpedo during the Naval Battle of Guadalcanal, killing all five brothers. From this incident came the "Sole Survivor Policy," meaning that the two Ehlers brothers had to be in separate outfits. Roland stayed in Company K of the 18th Infantry Regiment of the 1st Division, while Walter was transferred to Company L.

Despite the Sullivan rule, both of the brothers ended up on Omaha Beach on June 6, 1944, where Roland was killed instantly when his landing craft was struck by a German artillery shell. It was more than week later that Walter learned of the death of his brother.

Walter Ehlers faced almost certain death himself as he confronted the four Germans in the hedgerows with their guns pointed at him. In the words of Ehlers, however, "I shot them before they had a chance to react." The official citation for the Medal of Honor awarded to him for this action completes the story:

> Then crawling forward under withering machinegun fire, he pounced upon the gun crew and put it out of action. Turning his attention to two mortars protected by the crossfire of two machineguns, S/Sgt. Ehlers led his men through the hail of bullets to kill or put to flight the enemy of the mortar section, killing three men himself. After mopping up the mortar positions, he again advanced on a machinegun, his progress effectively covered by his squad. When he was almost on top of the gun, he leaped to his feet and, although greatly outnumbered, he knocked out the position single-handedly.

Second Lieutenant Walter D. Ehlers

In an action the following day, Ehlers was wounded in the back, but noticed his BAR man had been hit in the legs and arm.* Shooting the German sniper, he managed to carry the wounded rifleman to safety.

After the war, Walter Ehlers returned home to Kansas, and later moved west. He and his wife Dorothy live in Buena Park, California.

---

* BAR = Browning Automatic Rifle

CHEMICAL BANK & TRUST

ASSAULT ON MOUNT BELVEDERE

H. NEWCOMB ELDREDGE Veteran

"The entire front was on fire with artillery. You thought nobody could live under that concentration."

Newc Eldredge, on the bombardment of Germans on Hill 913 in the mountains of Italy, from an interview with *Veterans Chronicles*

February 19, 1945. The moon was rising in a clear sky as the men of the 10th Mountain Division prepared for the assault on Mount Belvedere, a strategic stronghold in the Apennine Mountains of Italy. As Private First Class Newc Eldredge of Company L in the 85th Infantry Regiment of the 10th Division recalled, the Apennines were "steep, rugged, and hard to maneuver around."

Capturing the summit of the mountain wouldn't be easy, and it was bound to be costly. For most of 4,000 feet up, the 10th would need to make its way through an icy darkness over terrain laced with barbwire and minefields, not to mention an enemy well dug in with artillery emplacements and machine gun nests. The 85th Regiment was given the steepest side of the mountain, and for Eldredge, the mission would be especially dangerous, for as lead scout, he had to crawl through minefields ahead of the others and cut the barbwire.

"Climb to Glory," the motto of the famed 10th Mountain Division, formed in 1943 to fight in the mountains of Italy.

One particular order they were given made the men especially nervous, and that was that they had to unload their guns and carry bayonets. No weapons were to be fired until after daylight, reportedly for two reasons. First, the attack was intended to be a surprise, and second, the flash from a fired weapon would give away the position of the attackers. The problem was, the setting off of mines soon alerted the Germans, who filled the sky with phosphorous flares that lit the landscape like daylight.

With the attack no longer a surprise, the bayonets were replaced by loaded weapons as the 10th worked its way up the mountain amidst exploding mortar shells and heavy rifle and machine gun fire. The 10th would lose more than 500 men that night. As the sun rose, bodies could be seen strewn all over the slope, frozen in death, some still in a firing position.

Newc Eldredge was born in Baltimore, Maryland, but was raised in Pittsford, New York. He went to the Pittsford School from the time he was in kindergarten. Eventually, he became interested in skiing, the school having built 20- and 35-meter jumps. He started jumping at eight or nine, and since he was at Pittsford through his senior year in high school, he had plenty of time to learn and practice.

Upon enlisting in the Army in November 1943, Eldredge volunteered for ski troops. First sent to Fort McClellan, Alabama, for basic training, he was finally able to join the 10th Mountain Division at Camp Hale, Colorado, in mid-1944. There, he and some 20,000 other volunteers were drilled in ice climbing, rappelling, snowshoeing, and winter combat, as well as skiing. After follow-on training at Camp Swift, Texas, Eldredge and the 10th were their way to Italy in November 1944.

The battle for Mount Belvedere and the surrounding ridges took four days of bloody, agonizing, uphill fighting, with Eldredge one of first to reach the top, having helped wipe out a couple of enemy machine gun nests along the way. Somehow, he managed to escape being wounded. But he was not so fortunate a couple of months later, as the 10th reached Hill 913 near Castel d'Aiano.

It was April 14th. From the valley, Eldredge could see the Germans were taking quite a pounding. "The entire front was on fire," but then as the 10th deployed up the mountain, it got quiet along the front. Suddenly, heavy machine gun fire came from the enemy, who had burrowed deep in foxholes during the American bombardment. Seeing tracer bullets aimed at his position, "from experience, you know mortars are going to be in on you very shortly," but before he and the men around him could escape fast enough under the machine gun fire, a shell detonated in the soft dirt between his feet, severely wounding him. With the help of a sergeant from another regiment, he managed to make it back to his lines and from there, to a field hospital.

For Eldredge, the war was over.

Once his wounds healed and he was discharged, Eldredge enrolled in Dartmouth College, where he was a member of the ski team

Private First Class H. Newcomb Eldredge

and chairman of the winter sports department. He then got married, and the couple soon moved to Colorado, where he studied for his graduate degree in history and teaching at Denver University.

When the Korean War broke out, Eldredge accepted a commission as a second lieutenant, serving initially as an intelligence officer and later as an infantry platoon officer while stationed in Colorado before being discharged a second time. He moved back to New England and opened his own insurance agency in Newport, New Hampshire.

Long retired from the business, Newc Eldredge and his wife Sally continue to reside in Newport.

EIGHTEEN HOURS IN MOGADISHU

MATTHEW EVERSMANN Veteran

"Before I was able to slide down the rope from the helicopter, one of my soldiers fell from the helicopter, fell off the rope. We figure about 60 feet to the ground. So we've got a casualty right off the bat."

Matt Eversmann, on the ill-fated mission to capture two lieutenants of Somali warlord Mohammed Farrah Aidid, from an interview with *Veterans Chronicles*

October 3, 1993. The mid-afternoon sky was clear and bright as the MH-60 helicopters crossed the city—a three- or four-minute journey from the small airport on the outskirts of Mogadishu, Somalia—and hovered over their destination. Operation Gothic Serpent was underway.

The intent of the mission was to capture two lieutenants of the Habr Gidr clan led by warlord Mohammed Farrah Aidid. The "snatch and grab" operation focused on a target building in the middle of the Barkara Market and was expected to take about 30 minutes. Each of the four Black Hawks would set down in the middle of the intersection and quickly disgorge a squad of Army Rangers assigned responsibility for blocking a corner of the square.

Four helicopters, four corners. Delta Force soldiers working with the Rangers would then drop down on the roof of the targeted building, clear it from the top down, and remove Aidid's henchmen. They would then all walk out to a point where they would be picked up by armored Humvees, which would convoy them out of the city.

The crew of Super Six-Four shortly before the Battle of Mogadishu: Winn Mahuron, Tommy Field, Bill Cleveland, Ray Frank, and Mike Durant. Super Six-Four was one of two Black Hawk helicopters to be shot down during the battle. Field, Cleveland, and Frank were killed in the action, with Durant being taken prisoner and held for 11 days.

For First Sergeant Matt Eversmann of the 3rd Battalion, 75th Ranger Regiment and leader of Chalk Four—which was responsible for blocking the northwest corner of the square—the problems began as his MH-60 neared its destination point. His helicopter was the last one coming in, and wash from the rotors stirred up so much dust that the pilot couldn't see to land. As a result, it had to hover short of the insertion point—about a block away—and the men had to slide some 60 feet down a rope to the ground. That was problem number one.

Problem number two was when it was Eversmann's turn to fast rope down through the cloud of dust and he discovered one of men crumpled up at the bottom. He had fallen off the rope. The good news was that the henchmen of Aidid they were seeking were in the building and were captured, along with 19 others who were also seized and processed, which took longer than anticipated.

Then, there was problem number three. All of a sudden, a Black Hawk went down a few blocks away... which changed the strategy for getting out of the city. The task force had to get over to it and rescue the men, which meant fighting their way from building to building, for the enemy stood between them and the downed helicopter. In minutes, what had been light erratic fire turned heavy, and from all directions.

Fortunately, Eversmann was well trained for the mission. Raised in rural Virginia, Eversmann worked for a bus factory while in high school. Afterwards, he attended Hampden-Sydney College near Farmville, Virginia, for three years before electing to enlist in the Army. As an infantryman, he was sent to Fort Drum, New York, with the 10th Mountain Division, which is where he was when the Gulf War broke out.

After his enlistment was up, Eversmann reenlisted and was assigned to the 3rd Battalion of the 75th Ranger Regiment at Fort Benning, Georgia. He spent the next eight and a half years as a career soldier in the Regiment in various capacities, including training with the British Parachute Regiment in the United Kingdom and time spent experiencing the harsh winters and mountainous terrain of Korea.

In August 1993, Eversmann was deployed to Mogadishu, Somalia, and he was now engaged in his seventh mission against the forces of Aidid, as he tried to reach the shot-down Super Six-One helicopter. Fortunately, the armored Humvees that were to transport them all out of the city showed up, and Eversmann was able to redirect them to the crash site and set up a perimeter.

The danger was far from over, though, for Chalk Four and a second Chalk, which had managed to join Eversmann, were surrounded and were undergoing intense fire from all directions by hundreds of the enemy. For 18 hours, Eversmann and the two Chalks managed to hold off the heavily armed Somalis. Finally, a 10th Mountain relief column was

First Sergeant Matthew Eversmann (right)

able to reach the site and evacuate the task force, along with the wounded men and the two pilots, both of whom had died in the crash.

All totaled, 18 soldiers were killed and 70 were wounded during the mission. More than 1,000 Somalis were dead.

Eversmann later spent 18 months in Iraq on active duty, where he led an Army Ranger force before retiring in 2008. He has lectured frequently at military bases and colleges across the U.S., and is currently a vice president of Allegeant in Timonium, Maryland.

Matt Eversmann and his wife Victoria reside in Baltimore, Maryland.

INSIDE THE PERIMETER AT BASTOGNE

RICHARD FALVEY Veteran

"I saw a plane explode in a ball of fire and, within seconds, another go down in front of me. All I could think was 'Dear Lord, let me out of this plane.' Those men never had a chance."

Red Falvey, on parachuting behind German lines during the early morning of D-Day, from an interview with *Veterans Chronicles*

December 24, 1944. It was bitter cold... well below zero. Heavy flakes of snow blown by the wind formed a white blanket on men and machinery and added to the foot or so already on the ground. All seven roads in and out of Bastogne, Belgium, had been cut off by the German army, and inside the perimeter, the Allied forces were tired, freezing, and out of food and medical supplies... not to mention the fact that they were outnumbered by the enemy surrounding them.

In his foxhole, Sergeant Richard "Red" Falvey had never been more hungry. Finally, during the day, he was given some bread and managed to put a couple of extra slices in his jacket for safekeeping. Because of the extreme weather and the heavy overcast sky, air drops had been impossible for days, and the men were slowly starving. They were less concerned about the Germans and weren't sure whether the lack of food or the numbing cold would get to them first. Food they could do nothing about, except to scrounge around empty supply boxes that once held K-rations, in case something had dropped on the ground. To combat the sub-zero temperatures, many wrapped burlap bags around their feet, and some had even gone to the extreme of cutting holes in their sleeping bags and walking around wearing them.

Paratroopers of the 101st Airborne Division watch as C-47s drop supplies over Bastogne, December 26, 1944.

Falvey was born in Yonkers, New York, and at the age of 21, joined the military, having made up his mind that he wanted to be jumping from planes. After training at Taccoa and Fort Benning, Georgia, he was assigned to the 2nd Battalion, Headquarters Company in the 506th

Parachute Infantry Regiment, which was part of the famed 101st Airborne Division. In the early morning of D-Day, he had been dropped into an apple orchard behind enemy lines on Normandy, six miles off target. "Everything was helter-skelter," Falvey once recalled in an interview with the Army War College. "Thirteen thousand men jumped into Normandy that morning, and we had an 11-minute window to jump everyone."

As the sky became gradually lighter, he and others of the 506th made their way to where they were supposed to be and managed both to secure the causeway and seize the high ground overlooking Utah Beach. From there, his unit fought through the hedgerows to Foucarville, first wiping out four 105mm howitzers raining artillery shells down on the men landing on Utah Beach, and later capturing the strategic town of Carentan.

After a respite of three months back in England, the 506th was dropped into Holland, seizing the Wilhelmina Bridges at Son, and from there moving south to capture Eindhoven with its four highway bridges over the Dommel River. They soon became familiar with such names as Saint Oedenrode, Uden, Veghel, Keovining, Nijmegen, Opheusden, and Randwigh, towns Falvey and the 506th fought through, at times, from house to house. By the end of November, they had reached the French artillery garrison outside the village of Mourmelon, where they rested and received replacements.

Next stop for the 101st was Bastogne, for the German army, in an opening round of the Battle of the Bulge, had surrounded the 28th Infantry Division, and the town was in danger of falling to three divisions of the XLVII Panzer Corps. On the 18th of December, the 101st fought its way into Bastogne and took up positions, organizing defenses, establishing a perimeter around the town, and blocking the roads that converge on Bastogne.

No air support, due to a lack of visibility, was possible, and the Allied forces inside the perimeter were forced to shift men, artillery fire, and tanks from place to place to fend off the probing actions and the Christmas Eve attack of the Panzers.

On Christmas Day, there was no break in the weather, but Falvey took the occasion to present the bread he had saved to friends with a "Merry Christmas."

Finally, Private Jake McNiece of the Pathfinders (see his story in this book) was able to set up a guidance signal for the 1,000 C-47s circling the town, and soon supplies of food, clothing, medical supplies, and ammunition were floating down through a clearing sky. On the 26th, elements of General George Patton's Third Army punched through the German lines and the siege was over.

Staff Sergeant Richard W. Falvey

After the war ended, Falvey returned home accompanying Hitler's and Goering's automobiles in a U.S. Treasury Department tour intended to sell savings bonds. Falvey and the tour traveled from the Pentagon in Virginia through the Southwest to Denver and back, stopping in towns and villages along the way. Afterward, he was employed as a brakeman and conductor by the New York Central Railroad.

Richard Falvey resides in Hammondsport, New York.

BASEBALL AND THE "LUCKY A"

ROBERT FELLER Veteran

"The Alabama *is the only ship in the 3rd Fleet that never lost a man to enemy action. We were always known as the 'Lucky A.'"*

Bob Feller, on the success and good fortune of the USS *Alabama*, despite heavy action in both the Europe and Pacific theaters, from an interview with *Veterans Chronicles*

Ted Williams, baseball's greatest hitter, once called Bob Feller "the fastest and best pitcher I ever saw during my career."* In 1941, Feller was 22 and in the prime of his baseball career with the Cleveland Indians. He had led the American League in wins in each of the last three seasons, and he had more strikeouts over the last four seasons than any other pitcher in either league. Feller had been in the majors for only five years, and yet he was already one of the most talked-about players in baseball. At 18, he had appeared on the cover of *Time* magazine and he even had a candy bar named after him.

The USS *Alabama* earned nine battle stars during World War II, seeing action in the Atlantic and Pacific theaters of war. She has been named a U.S. National Historical Landmark, and is permanently anchored in Mobile, Alabama.

Then, on December 7, 1941, the Japanese bombed Pearl Harbor. Two days later, Feller put professional baseball aside for a time and enlisted in the U.S. Navy. "Instead of signing my 1942 contract," Feller recalled, "I went over and swore in at the recruiting station in Chicago." Less than a month later, he reported for duty at the Norfolk Navy Yard in Portsmouth, Virginia.

Though at first he was slotted to be a physical training instructor, he wanted to be in combat, so he was sent to naval gunnery school in Newport, Rhode Island, and was then assigned to the battleship USS *Alabama* as a gun captain. His rank was that of chief petty officer.

"My battle station was on the 40mm quad on the port side aft." Feller's battery was supported by a crew of 24 men, and it consisted of a five-inch (38mm) dual-purpose gun, which was very effective both with

* Mark Feeney. "Bob Feller, 92, Hall of Famer had blazing fastball," *Boston Globe*, December 16, 2010.

standard shells and with what was called "Buck Rogers" ammunition; in other words, magnetic fuses. "If the bullet was going to miss the ship, it would explode and throw shrapnel."

In the early days of the war, young men—many under 18—from cities and farms across the nation flooded enlistment offices, anxious to fight the Nazis and especially the Japanese, who without warning had destroyed U.S. warships and aircraft and taken the lives of more than 2,400 Americans. Feller was no exception. He grew up with one thought and interest in mind, and that was to play baseball. But after Pearl Harbor, like for thousands of others, his priority became that of defending his country.

Raised on a farm near Van Meter Island, Feller started playing baseball as a very young boy in Bible School during summer vacations. From there, his life was filled with the national pastime, though grade school, through the American Legion, and through his first couple of years in high school, at which time he signed with the Cleveland Indians. He would finish high school in the off-season of 1936, receiving his diploma in the spring of 1937. His career, of course, is legendary, both before and after the war.

With baseball on hold, Feller headed out to sea with the *Alabama*. For several months in 1943, the battleship escorted convoys toting supplies for Russia through the frigid waters of the North Atlantic; and then, in July, it participated in Operation Governor, a diversion to draw German attention away from the planned Allied invasion of Sicily.

The *Alabama* also shelled the German battleship *Tirpitz* and tried to lure it from its lair at Fættenfjord, north of Trondheim, Norway, where it was camouflaged with trees and netting. The Germans refused to take the bait. British Lancaster bombers, however, finally got to the *Tirpitz* in November 1944. Two direct hits of 12,000-pound armor-piercing bombs caused a deck fire which spread rapidly to the ammunition magazine. Within minutes, the magazine exploded, blowing a large hole in the side of the ship, which then capsized and buried her superstructure on the bottom of the fjord.

In August 1943, after its encounter with the *Tirpitz*, the *Alabama* was detached from the British Home Fleet and departed for the Pacific, where over several months it participated in the Allied assault on the Japanese-held Gilbert Islands, landings on the atoll of

Chief Petty Officer Robert W. A. Feller

Tarawa, and the invasion of the Marshall Islands.

While the *Alabama* was later involved in screening air strikes and in bombing Japanese airfields on the Caroline Islands and the Philippines, Feller was transferred to inactive duty in August 1945, and two days afterward he rejoined the Cleveland Indians, where he resumed his record-setting baseball career.

Robert Feller passed away in Gates Mills, Ohio, on December 15, 2010.

SHUTTLING AMMUNITION AND BODIES WITH "DUCKS"

FREDERICK GRAY Veteran

"I had a brother serving in Europe. When I was headed for Iwo Jima, I received word he had been killed in Italy. I asked myself if I was going to be next."

Fred Gray, on the bloodiest fighting of the war awaiting him on Iwo Jima, from an interview with *Veterans Chronicles*

He drove a "duck." Officially, it was called a DUKW… *D* signifying the production code for 1942, *U* for amphibious utility truck, *K* for front-wheel drive, and *W* for the two rear-wheel driving axles. It plowed through the water like a boat, it drove like a truck on land, and it was a "sitting duck" for Japanese machine guns and artillery on the beaches of Iwo Jima.

"It had six wheels, and you could inflate and deflate the tires, as you needed to, while you're operating the truck," recalled Fred Gray, who had been assigned to the 476th Amphibious Truck Company, an all-black outfit attached to the 4th Marine Division. As tough as it was for the infantry landing on the Japanese stronghold, gaining the beach was only half of Gray's problem. He had to go back again to the ships, for the job of the ducks was to ferry supplies, including ammunition, from the ships to the shore, and to evacuate the men wounded during the battle for the island. A hit on his duck while moving in toward the beach at its top speed of six miles per hour could possibly blow him sky high.

African-American DUKW drivers join the battle for Iwo Jima as riflemen after their vehicle was destroyed by enemy fire during the initial invasion, February 19, 1945.

Gray was born and raised in St. Leonard, Maryland. He grew up in a segregated section of the rural community and attended a one-room schoolhouse through the eighth grade. Since there was no high school for blacks where he lived, he went to work for his father, who constructed houses and barns and other buildings wherever he could find work.

In 1941, Gray's brother Norman was drafted into the all-black 92nd

Army Infantry Division, but since Fred was only 16 at the time, it wasn't until 1943 that he received his draft notice. He left home for Fort Meade, Maryland, and was then shipped to Camp Gardiner Johnson in Tallahassee, Florida, for basic training. At the time, the military was as segregated as the nation as a whole. In Florida, the presence of blacks led to trouble between the black and white soldiers. Jim Crow laws prevented the black soldiers from entering the USO and other facilities on the base.* "It was demoralizing, very demoralizing," Gray once reported.

In Florida, the tension between black and white troops led to fighting and eventually a race riot. Gray and others were subsequently sent to an Army camp in Seattle, Washington, and from there, on to Hawaii for six to eight weeks of additional training with the 4th Marine Division.

In February 1945, Gray was on the high seas headed for the Japanese-held island of Iwo Jima when he got word that Norman had been killed in September in Northern Italy. He wondered if he was next.

For Gray, piloting his duck boat back and forth between the ships and the beach at Iwo Jima was pure hell. Pools of blood oozed down through the volcanic ash and body parts littered the beach. Many of the bodies, mangled and mutilated, could not be identified. Then there was the wounded. Loading them onto stretchers and transporting them out to the hospital ship was a gut-wrenching, never-ending job, one that went on for 36 days.

Unlike many of his friends, some whom he had gotten close to, Gray managed to survive Iwo Jima and the war unscathed. Why or how he is not sure, for he managed to run his duck boat back and forth, carrying ammunition to the troops while under constant fire. The bravery of the men of the 476th was so recognized and appreciated that the Marines on the beach and in the foxholes would cheer the boats and their drivers as they moved inland. Gray figured that about half of the men in his company made it back to the States.

Gray's service on Iwo Jima was so exceptional that he was offered the opportunity to attend Officer Candidate School (OCS), but he declined, as he had decided not to pursue a military career. He returned home and went back to work for his father. He graduated from high school and was later accepted into the Washington, DC Police Academy. After six years as a policeman, he joined the National Park Service, retiring after a 34-year career. He was the founder of the Black Iwo Jima Veterans Association.

Frederick Gray passed away in Columbia, Maryland, on August 10, 2009, his wife Helen surviving him.

First Sergeant Frederick D. Gray

* Jim Crow laws were state and local laws passed in the South between 1876 and 1975 that had the effect of maintaining segregation between the white and black races. "Jim Crow" was a derisive term used in reference to laws that pertained to "Negroes."

FLIGHT OF THE "WHIRLING DERVISH"

THOMAS GRIFFIN Veteran

"We assigned specific targets to each crew, exactly where they were to go, and even a secondary target in case of weather or the enemy prevented them from hitting the original target."

Tom Griffin, on the secret planning for the Doolittle Raid, from an interview with *Veterans Chronicles*

He had been sent to Washington to get the maps for the raid. Army Air Force Major Thomas Griffin, a navigator with the 17th Bombardment Group, recalled the mission's extreme need for secrecy. "If any information at all got out, which would alert the Japanese that such plans were in the offing, we would never get there."

For this reason, during the week, as Griffin and fellow officer Captain (later Major) David Jones were picking up and going over the maps of Japan and China, "Air Force intelligence changed the lock on the door of one of the offices, and we did all our talking and planning about the raid in this locked room that [only] we had the keys to."

The mission would be the first of its kind, with the Army Air Force contributing medium-range bombers and trained crews, and the Navy providing the aircraft carrier, in this case, the USS *Hornet*. The target: cities, airfields, and industries in Japan. Commanding the mission would be Lieutenant Colonel James H. Doolittle, an aviation pioneer and daredevil flyer in the 1920s and '30s. The bomber he chose was the B-25, and his crews would be volunteers willing to take on an important and dangerous mission against the enemy without being told what it was all about.

The intent was to shock the Japanese military, which was convinced that their homeland was safe from Allied attacks, for they believed—with good reason—it couldn't be reached by either air or sea. It would also force the Japanese to keep fighter planes at home, rather than disbursing them elsewhere in

B-25 Mitchell bombers are prepped on the deck of the USS *Hornet* in advance of the Doolittle Raid on Tokyo, April 18, 1942.

the Pacific. Then, too, the raid would almost certainly boost the morale of Americans after the devastating attack on Pearl Harbor.

There were two problems, however. First, the bombers had to be launched within 400 or so miles of Japan in order for the aircraft to reach their targets and then have enough fuel to fly on to landing fields in China, where they could refuel. The second problem was that the planes had only 500 feet of deck on the *Hornet* from which to take off, and no B-25 had ever done that before.

But the biggest problem was an unexpected setback. The *Hornet* and its task force, including the USS *Enterprise* with Admiral William Halsey, Jr. commanding, was deep within Japanese-controlled waters, but still some 750 miles out from the mainland of Japan, when on April 17, 1942, they were spotted by two Japanese fishing vessels. The boats were quickly sunk by fighter planes from the *Enterprise*, but had they been able to radio a warning message off to Japan? Halsey couldn't take a chance, and sent word to the *Hornet*: "Tell the Doolittle boys to take off immediately."

While the 80 crewmembers onboard the 16 B-25s had mixed feelings about whether or not they could get the planes off the *Hornet* and into the air, they all knew to the last man that the planes weren't going to make it back. They would run out of fuel, and all 16 would be lost. Those who survived a crash landing would most likely become prisoners.

For Griffin, who was born in Green Bay, Wisconsin, and had begun his military career as a second lieutenant after graduating from the University of Alabama's ROTC program, being a navigator on a bomber in the Pacific was a far cry from the year he spent in the coast artillery.

The first in line was Doolittle, and he made it off the carrier into the stiff wind that raked the ship, giving hope to the men in the planes lined up behind him. The ninth plane to take off was Griffin's. Fortunately, his plane, the "Whirling Dervish," made it into the air, and hours later, it was over Toyko, though by the time it reached there, the Japanese were ready for them and the sky was filled with flak.

After dropping their bombs, the pilot, Lieutenant Doc Watson, turned southwest toward China, flying through fog and rain. By some miracle, the fuel held out until the B-25 was about 300 miles into China before the engines began sputtering. Jumping into the night at 10,000 feet,

Major Thomas C. Griffin

Griffin had no idea what to expect, but his parachute ended up getting hung up on the top of a bamboo tree. Rescued and welcomed as a hero by the Chinese, he was eventually flown to India and then back to the U.S. He was later shot down over Sicily, and spent 22 months in a prison camp.

After the war, Thomas Griffin had his own accounting business before retiring in 1983.

Today, he lives in Cincinnati, Ohio, his wife Esther having passed away a few years ago.

EIGHT HUNDRED YARDS OF HELL

RALPH GRIFFITHS Veteran

"The old-timers didn't think it would be that tough… 800 yards across the beach is all it was. 'We'll have that mountain in our hands in two hours.' Little did they know it would take about 800 casualties and four days."

Ralph Griffiths, on the raising of the flag on Iwo Jima, from an interview with *Veterans Chronicles*

The 40 men of Easy Company were crawling on their hands and knees toward the top of Mount Suribachi, more than 500 feet above sea level. The fighting had been so intense getting across the beach to the base of the mountain that Private Ralph Griffiths of the 2nd Platoon, 28th Regiment, 5th Marine Division had no idea what to expect at the top. Most likely, the Japanese would be defending it even more fiercely than they had below, and Griffiths knew his chances of making it back down the mountain could be slim.

The invasion force consisting of three divisions of U.S. Marines had landed on Iwo Jima on February 19, 1945, and the resistance had been light—at first. The Japanese plan was to hold back in unleashing heavy fire on the Americans until the beach was filled with Marines and equipment. Then all hell broke loose.

Fire is concentrated on Japanese positions on Mount Suribachi, the enemy stronghold on the southern tip of Iwo Jima.

Part of the problem facing the Marines was that the defenders were holed up in caves and bunkers with an elaborate network of underground tunnels and trenches connecting cleverly concealed gun emplacements. The Japanese themselves were seldom seen… at least alive. From out of nowhere, machine gun nests would open up, raking the American troops; sharpshooters would take aim from the blackness of caves; and artillery, ensconced in bunkers with reinforced steel doors, would rain down shells, only to pull back and disappear into the caves of Mount Suribachi to the south or the rocky terrain to the north. And even when the Americans would take out a cave or pillbox, shooting would erupt minutes later as other Japanese defenders would slip back in using a connecting tunnel.

The fight to the top had been slow and tedious, but in reaching the summit, Griffiths and the men of Easy Company were in for a surprise.

Griffiths was born in Girard, Ohio, and raised in Youngstown, quitting high school after his junior year in order to join the service. Since he was only 17, he needed to have his parents' permission. A bigger obstacle was that he had to weigh 112 pounds to get in, and he weighed only 104. He was sent home and told to eat bananas. Fortunately, he worked at a market and was paid in food instead of cash. "They gave me a whole stock of bananas. I must have eaten 60 bananas in a week and a half," Griffiths recalled. Back at the recruiting station, he was asked, "Did you eat the bananas?" When told "Yes," the recruiter said, "Okay, 112."

Griffiths was sent to San Diego, California, for eight weeks of boot camp and training, and from there, he spent six months at Camp Pendleton, California, where he was assigned to Easy Company in the newly formed 5th Marine Division. It was then on to Camp Tarawa in Hawaii. Here—though Griffiths didn't know it at the time—the 5th Division was to be trained for the invasion of Iwo Jima. In the words of Griffiths, Easy Company was made up in part of former raiders and paratroopers, hardened men from disbanded units and "as tough as they would come."

Reaching the top of Mount Suribachi, the patrol couldn't believe it was undefended, and shortly after, six men raised the first flag. As is well recorded, the flag was soon replaced with a larger flag, the five Marines and the Navy corpsman raising it becoming immortalized by the historic photograph taken by Associated Press photographer Joe Rosenthal.

As events proved, far more dangerous than the top of the mountain was its sides, and Easy Company was sent to circle the mountain. In reaching the south side, all Griffiths could see in front of him was ocean and the U.S. destroyers. Seeking some relief from the Japanese firing on them, he was led by two of the men who had raised the second flag—Sergeant Michael Strank and Corporal Harlon Block—into an "alcove" considered to be safe.

Minutes later, a shell landed 20 feet in front of them, killing Strank and Block and hitting Griffiths with shrapnel and blinding him for three days with sand. For him, the battle was over, and the next day, March 1st, he was headed back to Guam, where he was hospitalized for six and a half weeks. After that, he returned to his unit and was greeted by the men he had fought with. Only 31 of the original 310 were left.

Corporal Ralph K. Griffiths

After the war, Griffiths returned home and went to work for a steel mill in Niles, Ohio, and later was a food broker for companies in Youngstown and Warren, Ohio.

Ralph Griffiths and his wife Florence reside in Girard, Ohio.

AVENGING HIS BROTHER'S DEATH

WILLIAM GUARNERE Veteran

"The Germans were as scared as we were. They didn't know where we were at, and we didn't know where they were at."

"Wild Bill" Guarnere, on jumping into Normandy during the early morning hours of D-Day, from an interview with *Veterans Chronicles*

He missed the church by 400 or 500 yards, jumping well beyond his intended DZ (drop zone)... which put him in middle of the enemy, for on the early morning of D-Day, June 6, 1944, the Germans occupied Ste-Mère-Église. Sergeant William Guarnere of the 101st Airborne, and those in Easy Company who jumped with him, may have been the only Allied forces around, for the 82nd Airborne, scheduled to take the town, hadn't yet touched down.

Somehow, Guarnere moved off in the darkness and the company gradually came together with its commanding officer, Lieutenant Richard Winters. The job of Easy Company of the 506th Parachute Infantry Regiment was to secure the village of Ste-Marie-du-Mont and the causeway leading up from Utah Beach. The intent was to prevent the enemy from reinforcing troops manning the bunkers and artillery emplacements and to capture Germans who might be retreating from the beach defenses.

Paratroopers awaiting the signal to jump. More than 20,000 Allied paratroopers would make the jump behind enemy lines on D-Day, June 6, 1944.

Guarnere was more than ready to fight the Germans. The day before D-Day, he was told his brother had been killed in Italy. "It hit me with a brick," he noted. "I was like a crazy man."

He was soon being called "Wild Bill"... and with good reason. He made it his personal mission to kill as many of the enemy as he could. Lieutenant Winters found this out soon after Guarnere caught up with him on the 6th. As the unit headed south toward Ste-Marie-du-Mont, a German supply platoon was heard coming toward them. Winters pulled the men off the road and set up an ambush, instructing them to wait for his order to fire. Guarnere, however, anxious to begin the process of avenging his brother's death, opened up on the Germans, killing most of them.

Guarnere was born and raised in South Philadelphia, Pennsylvania, in what he termed as a "hard-scrabble" life. "We came from a family of ten kids. It was a tough life. I thought we were going to end up in jail when we were kids." To get away from that life, he joined the Citizens Military Training Camp (CMTC) program. Though he was only 15 at the time, he got his mother to sign papers stating that he was 17. Unfortunately, after the third year, the program was cancelled, and he ended up back on a street corner, hanging around.

After Pearl Harbor, Guarnere left high school before graduation and went to work for Baldwin Locomotive Works, making Sherman tanks. Eventually, he switched his work schedule to nights and completed high school. On August 31, 1942, Guarnere enlisted in the paratroops and went through basic training at Camp Toccoa, Georgia, before being assigned to Easy Company.

His first combat jump was over Normandy… and by mistake, into Ste-Mère-Église.

After several weeks of assaulting German positions in Normandy, including the capture and dismantling of 105mm howitzers at Brécourt Manor, Easy Company was returned to England to prepare for a jump into Paris. Instead, a decision was made for the 506th to jump into Holland for the opening campaign of Operation Market Garden, a failed strategy—for a number of reasons—to capture key bridges across canals and, ultimately, the Rhine River. If successful, an Allied thrust into the industrial heartland of Germany was expected to end the war by Christmas 1944. That never happened, for Operation Market Garden was abandoned.

In mid-October 1944, the war could have been over for Guarnere, for he was shot in the right leg by a sniper while driving a motorcycle he had stolen from a farmer to check on the men of his platoon, which was spread along a line of about a mile on the south side of the Rhine. The shot fractured his right tibia and resulted in shrapnel being lodged in his right buttock. Evacuated to a hospital in England to recover, he ended up walking out of the hospital to return on his own to Easy Company, but was caught, court-martialed, and demoted to a private. (The papers never came through, so he remained a private first class in rank.)

Staff Sergeant William J. Guarnere

Threatening to go AWOL again if he wasn't sent back to his company, Guarnere got his way and was returned to Easy Company in the Netherlands in time to be convoyed into Bastogne to help prevent the capture of the city during the Battle of the Bulge.

Guarnere later lost his leg during an artillery barrage, while trying to help a wounded friend. For him, the war was finally over.

Over the years, William Guarnere has held a number of jobs, and is active in veterans' organizations. He continues to reside in South Philadelphia.

BLAZING A TRAIL... IN THE SKY

ELAINE DANFORTH HARMON Veteran

"Other than flying or ferrying as a group, towing targets, and test flying of planes that had just been repaired, one of the most dangerous things you could do is fly an airplane right after it's been manufactured."

Elaine Harmon, on the dangers of flying during the war as a Women Airforce Service Pilot (WASP), from an interview with *Veterans Chronicles*

She knew her mother wouldn't want her to fly. So she asked her father. At the time, Elaine Harmon was attending the University of Maryland, and the school offered the Civilian Pilot Training Program (CPTP). She was underage, so she needed his approval, and sent the request to his office. "I got it right back with a signature and the $40." Her mother never knew she flew while she was in college. "I think we avoided a divorce."

While her mother may not have been pleased to learn her daughter was flying while in school, Harmon's focus in college remained on getting her degree, and she ended up graduating with a bachelor of science in microbiology and working for a while in a Baltimore, Maryland hospital on contagious diseases.

Some 25,000 women applied to join the WASP program in World War II. Of them, only 1,830 were accepted and took the oath, with 1,074 passing training and officially joining the outfit.

Then, Pearl Harbor happened. Married by now, she moved around the country with her husband, taking jobs in hospital laboratories, working on preparing serum. He wanted to help out in the war effort, but was ineligible for the draft, for he was 4F. However, in May 1944, after American forces captured the island of Biak from the Japanese, he went to work for a company that repaired aircraft instruments, setting up a workshop on the airbase there, so that U.S. aircraft could be repaired in an hour or two in the Pacific theater instead of being sent back to the States.

For Elaine Harmon, it was time for her to do her part, so she joined the Women Airforce Service Pilots (WASP) program at age 24, which was easier said than done, for of the 25,000 women who applied, 1,830 were accepted and took the oath, and out of these, only 1,074 got through the training. She graduated from WASP flight training in September 1944 at Avenger Field in Sweetwater, Texas.

Instrumental in the formation of WASP were two women: Jackie Cochran, a national speed record champion, who started a group known as the Women's Flying Training Detachment (WFTD), and Nancy Harkness Love, who began the Women's Auxiliary Ferrying Squadron (WAFS). In August 1943, the two organizations were merged into the WASP program.

The idea of the Women Airforce Service Pilots program was to free male pilots for combat missions by using women pilots to ferry aircraft from factories to military bases, instruct pilots in instrumentation flying, and tow drones and aerial targets. From September 1943 to December 1944, when the program was disbanded, the WASPs would log more than 60 million miles.

The WASP program was sanctioned by Lieutenant General Henry "Hap" Arnold, chief of the Army Air Forces, and though the women pilots were trained to fly "the Army way" and were stationed at 120 airbases across the U.S., flying all types of military aircraft—including the latest off the production lines—the program was not part of the military, and the WASPs received no benefits. "We paid for our own housing," Harmon recalled. "We didn't have a uniform... so we started wearing tan slacks with a white shirt. That was our uniform."

The disparity in treatment by the Army was so flagrant, the 38 women pilots who lost their lives in service to their country were sent home at their family's expense and without traditional military honors. "One was a tow target pilot. Her plane caught fire. She landed it ok, but she couldn't get the hood open. The lock was jammed, and she just sat in there and burned to death." The Army wouldn't even allow the draping of an American flag on the coffins of the deceased.

Harmon, a pioneer in the WASP program, spent most of service time training male pilots on instrument flying. "I would take the plane up and land it, but while in the air, he would go under the hood [fly on instruments]. I had to make sure he didn't run into a mountain or go into a spin..." For most of her career in the service, Harmon was stationed at Nellis Air Force Base in Las Vegas, Nevada.

With the disbanding of the program, Harmon returned to Baltimore, Maryland, and then went

First Lieutenant Elaine D. Harmon

to California to work as an air traffic controller. After the war, she settled in Silver Spring, Maryland, with her husband and raised a family.

Finally, after hundreds of former WASPs lobbied Congress and collected signatures across the country, the G.I. Bill Improvement Act of 1977 was enacted, granting the WASP corps full military status for their service. Then, on July 1, 2009, President Barack Obama and Congress awarded the WASP program the Congressional Gold Medal.

Elaine Harmon continues to reside in Silver Spring, Maryland.

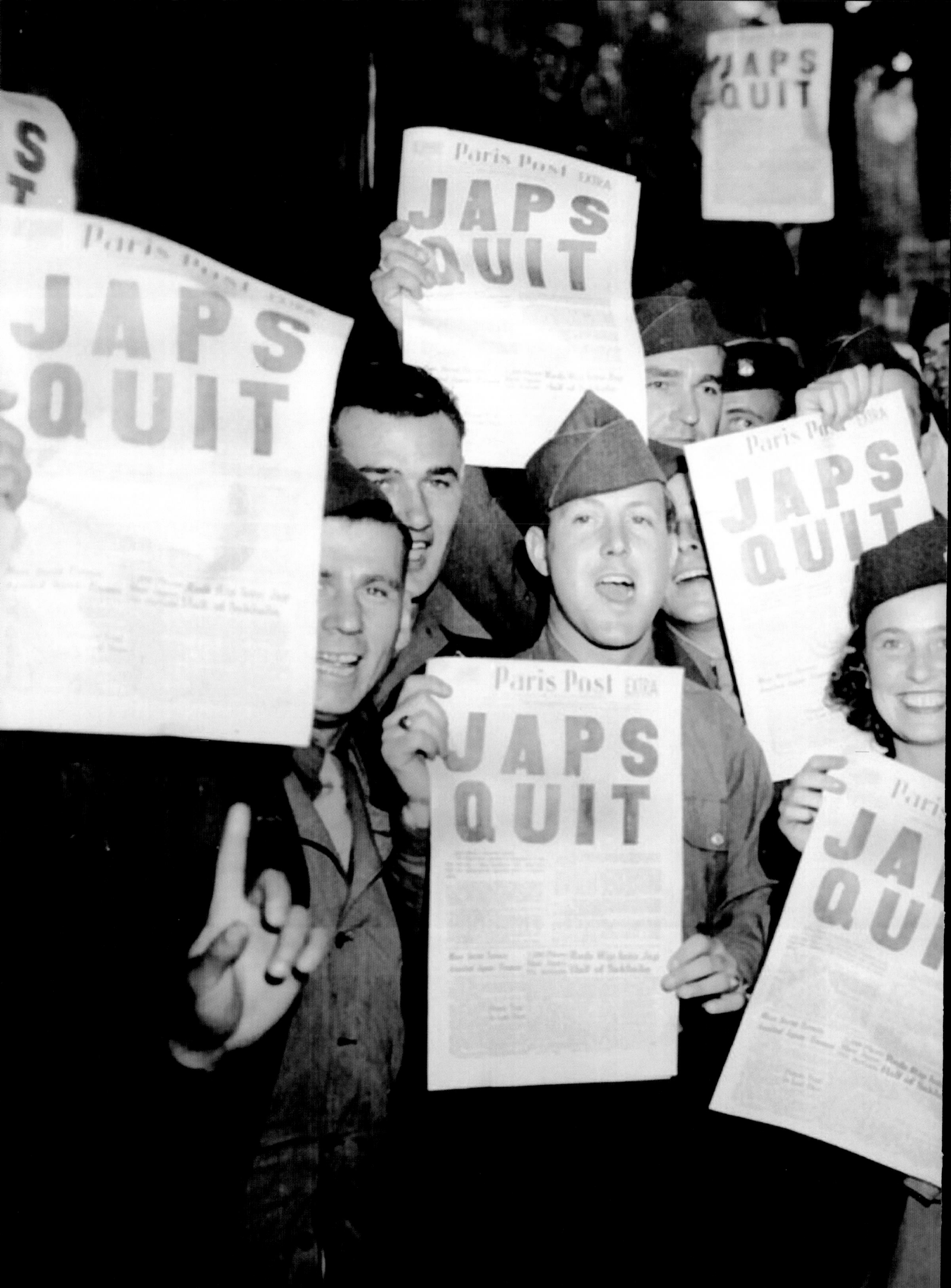

Paris Post EXTRA

JAPS QUIT

Paris Post
JAPS
QUIT

FIGHT TO HOLD HELL'S HIGHWAY

EDWARD HEFFRON Veteran

"Every morning, we would come out of those apple orchards and open up 'Hell's Highway' again. We were up there for 70-some days."

Babe Heffron, on efforts by the 101st Airborne to keep a critical road in the Netherlands open during the Battle of Market Garden, from an interview with *Veterans Chronicles*

On D-Day, he was still in England, but not for long. After the successful landings in Normandy, the 101st Airborne returned to England to prepare for its next mission: a massive, risky, and ultimately costly Allied thrust into Germany that became known as Operation Market Garden. For Private First Class Edward "Babe" Heffron of the 506th Parachute Infantry Regiment in the 101st, parachuting out of a C-47 over northern Holland was his first combat jump of the war.

September 17, 1944. The first objective of the 506th was to secure the bridge over the Wilhelmina Canal in the Netherlands. Landing near the town of Son, the 2nd and 3rd Battalions—including Babe Heffron, machine gunner in the 2nd—methodically cleared the village, while the 1st Battalion fought its way through enemy fire toward the canal. As the

Men of E Company, 506th Parachute Infantry Regiment—today known as "The Band of Brothers"—in World War II. "Babe" Heffron can be seen squatting in the very front row, second from left.

three battalions jointly approached the bridge, the Germans blew it up.

Valuable hours had been lost, but eventually, elements of the 506th made it across the canal and took out the enemy on the other side of what had been the bridge. The following day, the regiment moved south and liberated the town of Eindhoven. Further north, the British 1st Airborne Division was jumping into Arnhem. Opening the road between Eindhoven and Arnhem would be critical to the combined Allied effort. At Son, British engineers were hurriedly working on building a Bailey bridge over the Wilhelmina Canal to enable the movement of tanks and heavy equipment across the canal.

Despite the delay caused by the loss of the bridge, the 506th had completed its initial objectives, but the toughest fighting lay ahead, for it now had the job of protecting the dikes and keeping open the ribbon of road the 101st came to call "Hell's Highway."

Growing up in South Philadelphia, Heffron did what he felt he had to do to help his family survive, from stealing coal out of railway cars for heat at home to hustling on the streets for whatever he could scrounge up for nickels and dimes. He attended South Philadelphia High School, but had to drop out to earn money during the Depression.

When he heard about Pearl Harbor, "I was down in old man Marker's candy store." He and his friends had built a dance hall over the store. "I went upstairs, pulled the juke box cord out, and said, 'Fellas, girls, there will no more dancing today. We all know what we have to do. The Japanese bombed Pearl Harbor.'" No one knew where Pearl Harbor was, but that didn't matter. America had been attacked and the country was at war.

In August, Heffron was able to enlist, but had to wait to be called up. In the interim, he worked seven days a week as a civilian sandblaster of aircraft carriers at the shipyard in Camden, New Jersey. Three months later, he was called up and sent to Fort Eustis, Virginia, and ultimately began his training for the U.S. Airborne. In September 1943, he was on a transport ship to England, where he continued his training until his chance to jump in combat came with the invasion of the Netherlands during Operation Market Garden.

After opening its assigned portion of Hell's Highway, the 506th came under heavy fire and took severe casualties, as the Germans launched counterattacks daily to cut the road and prevent the movement of Allied forces. In the meantime, the British 1st Airborne Division encountered far stronger resistance from the enemy at Arnhem than anticipated and had to be withdrawn. While Market Garden turned out to be a failed operation, it did help the Allies to establish a foothold that months later led to crossing of the Rhine River and penetration into the industrial heartland of Germany.

For the 101st Airborne and the 506th Regiment, the next mission was to relieve the 28th Infantry Division, surrounded by enemy forces at Bastogne in the opening phase of the Battle of the Bulge. As Heffron recalled, "The weather was terrible... 26 or 27 degrees below zero." They had no winter clothing and were low on food, ammunition, and medical supplies. Fortunately, on Christmas Day, the weather cleared and skies were filled with parachutes dropping supplies from circling C-47s. Finally, General George Patton's Third Army broke through to relieve the siege.

Heffron fought his way through Germany with the 506th, all the way to the capture of Hitler's Eagle Nest. After the war, he worked for a whiskey distillery plant in Philadelphia, and when it moved, he spent the next 27 years working on the city's waterfront.

Babe Heffron and his wife Delores continue to reside in Philadelphia, Pennsylvania.

CRASH-LANDING AT CHOSIN, ON PURPOSE

THOMAS HUDNER, JR. Veteran

"I made one pass over Jesse's airplane to get a feel for how the airplane would be, dropped all of my ordinance, my rockets and bombs, and fired off all my gun ammunition to get as light as possible."

Tom Hudner, on crash-landing his plane to save fellow pilot Jesse Brown, who had been shot down, from an interview with *Veterans Chronicles*

By early December 1950, American forces in Korea were pushing up toward China, and were 70 or 80 miles south of Manchuria and the Yalu River, which separated China from North Korea. Then, almost without warning, some 100,000 Chinese troops swarmed across the Yalu to attack the contingent of U.S. Army and Marine forces near the mountainous countryside of the Chosin Reservoir. Providing close air support as the heavily outnumbered Americans attempted to fall back was pilot Tom Hudner and Fighter Squadron 32, flying Corsair fighter-bombers from the carrier USS *Leyte*.

Mrs. Daisy Brown, widow of Ensign Jesse Brown, congratulates Lieutenant Junior Grade Thomas J. Hudner, Jr. upon his being awarded the Medal of Honor.

Taking a hit from ground fire was fellow pilot Jesse Brown, who radioed that he had lost power and was looking for a place to land. One of the pilots in the squadron noticed a small clearing on the side of a snowy mountain. Directed to it, Brown attempted to glide in over the treetops. "When he hit the ground," recalled Hudner, "he hit it with such force the aircraft actually buckled at the cockpit." He continued, "There was no question in the minds of any of us but that he perished in the airplane."

But then something happened. As the squadron flight leader radioed for helicopter assistance, the canopy of the downed aircraft opened. Brown was still alive.

There wasn't enough time to wait for the helicopter, however, for smoke was pouring from the cowling. The plane was on fire. Without hesitation, Hudner made the decision to rescue his friend. But do so, he would need to crash-land his own plane. To lessen the probability of an explosion on impact, he dropped his bombs and ammunition, and braced himself for what was coming.

Raised in Fall River, Massachusetts, Hudner went through grade school, junior high, and a year of parochial school before deciding that he wanted to attend Philips Academy in Andover, Massachusetts, where his father had gone. His grandfather was an Irish immigrant who had started a meat and grocery business with a horse-drawn wagon that Hudner's father grew into a number of successful markets in the Fall River area.

After completing his education at the U.S. Naval Academy, Ensign Hudner decided that he wanted to be a naval air pilot. The war was over, the demand for pilots was less, and the Navy had a requirement that candidates for aviation or submarines had to spend two years on a ship. In Hudner's case, he was assigned as a communications watch officer and as the signal officer to a new heavy cruiser.

Finally, his orders came through for flight training, and he got his wings in August 1949.

When the Korean War broke out, Hudner was on an aircraft carrier in the Mediterranean. He had no idea where Korea was. But he soon found out.

Hudner's plan was to pull Brown from the plane before it exploded in flames and wait for the helicopter, assuming he got down safely himself. The mountain on which he hoped to land had an upslope of 20 or 30 degrees and was covered in a couple of feet of snow. He would fly parallel to the slope with the wheels up and let himself settle down into the slope. It didn't quite work out that way… "I came down pretty hard." But he made it.

The downed plane was only smoldering, but unfortunately, Hudner couldn't get Brown out, as his legs were pinned inside the fuselage. He needed help and repeated the call for the helicopter. When the helicopter pilot arrived, the two of them together still couldn't free Brown. As darkness came on, the helicopter had to return to base, as it didn't have the instrumentation to fly at night. Hudner was forced to leave the now unconscious pilot behind, knowing there was nothing he could do for him and that if he stayed, neither would be likely to survive the sub-zero temperatures of the night.

Hudner was taken first to a small Marine camp at Chosin Reservoir, from which the Marines were withdrawing, and after three days of bad weather in which planes couldn't fly, he was returned to the *Leyte*. He had begged to be returned to his friend, but was not allowed to because of the possibility of an ambush. He later learned that the decision was made to cremate Brown in the cockpit of his plane by dropping a napalm bomb on it, as well as Hudner's plane. As far as Hudner knows, the remains are still there.

Captain Thomas J. Hudner, Jr.

During the war, Hudner held a number of positions in the Navy, and was executive officer of the USS *Kitty Hawk* supercarrier for a short time during the Vietnam War. He retired in 1973 and worked as a management consultant in civilian life and with various veterans' organizations.

Thomas Hudner and his wife Georgea reside in Concord, Massachusetts.

LEAPFROGGING TO LUZON

ERNEST HUETER Veteran

"I was transferred to Intelligence on General MacArthur's staff and was responsible for studying the beaches for a landing at Kagoshima Bay on the Japanese homeland. We projected that on D-Day plus one, we would probably suffer 100,000 casualties."

Ernie Hueter, on the costly task facing the Allies in attacking the Japanese mainland, from an interview with *Veterans Chronicles*

It was going to take thousands of boats and thousands of coxswains. Where was the U.S. going to get them? This was the problem facing Second Lieutenant Ernest Hueter of the newly formed Engineer Amphibian Command (EAC). Invasions by land meant beaches, and they, in turn, meant finding a means of ferrying men onto the beaches from transports offshore.

Unfortunately, neither the Army nor the Navy had any experience to speak of with small landing craft, the type that would carry men, as opposed to tanks and heavy equipment. For Hueter, the search was on, and he toured the East Coast, marina after marina, looking for people experienced in seamanship and navigation. To solve the boat problem, the answer had to be the Higgins boat, which was already being supplied to the British and used in commando raids.

The LCVP—better known as the Higgins boat—was used extensively in amphibious landings in World War II, and could carry a platoon-sized complement of 36 men.

The problem with the Higgins boat was that equipment had to be unloaded and the soldiers had to disembark over the sides, thus increasing their exposure to enemy fire. After a series of modifications, a design evolved in which its two machine guns were moved to the rear of the boat, enabling a full-width ramp to be built in the front for unloading the troops. The new design was designated an LCVP (Landing Craft, Vehicle, Personnel).

Born and raised in San Francisco, Hueter could have had no idea as to his future career in the Army. His interest was in horses, and he had convinced his father to allow him to attend the New Mexico Military Institute, which was a cavalry school. Only 18 at the time he graduated—he had to wait until he was 21 to be an officer in the Army—he went on to attend the University of Missouri.

After graduating in 1942, now 21 and eligible to be an officer, Hueter quickly learned that the military had no use for horses, and he accepted a commission in the EAC. "I was assigned to that because I used to race boats and was an Olympic-class swimmer," Hueter observed in an interview with *Veterans Chronicles*.

With the Higgins boats he needed, Hueter began training at Camp Edwards on Cape Cod, Massachusetts, and then on the beaches of Martha's Vineyard, Massachusetts, before transporting boats and men on a troop train to Carabelle, Florida. Final training came at Fort Ord on Monterey Bay, California, in preparation for the upcoming invasions of the islands held by the Japanese.

It was there that Hueter tested and demonstrated a brand new amphibious vehicle called the DUKW, soon referred to as the "duck" by the soldiers. "They were clumsy and slow, underpowered, and they could not handle a surf of any kind," Hueter recalled. Because of their ability to drive up on the beaches and across the sand, though, he would see they played a major role in jockeying supplies in to the troops onshore and in ferrying the wounded back to the ships offshore.

As is well recorded, thanks to the training and organization of Hueter's command, the LCVPs were singularly responsible for successfully landing tens of thousands of Allied soldiers, not only on the shores of islands in the Pacific held by the Japanese, but also on the beaches of Normandy. Supreme Allied Commander Dwight D. Eisenhower, in fact, declared that the Higgins boats were crucial to the Allied victory on the European western front.

In the Pacific, the Allied forces leapfrogged from island to island, slowly driving the Japanese from the Solomons with Hueter participating in 24 invasions. By the time the Allied invasions reached the shores of Luzon with General Douglas MacArthur's return to the Philippines, Hueter had a new job. He was the deputy beach commander at White Beach. But it was only temporary. He was soon on MacArthur's staff, engaged in intelligence work for G2. His job was that of studying the beaches for a landing on the Japanese homeland at Kagoshima Bay. He estimated that the Allied forces would suffer 100,000 casualties during the landing.

Major Ernest B. Hueter

The dropping of atomic bombs on Hiroshima and Nagasaki ended the need for further planning.

Hueter returned home to pursue a distinguished career in top management of Interstate Brands and as president of the National Legal Center for the Public Interest. He also held high-level volunteer posts in numerous national organizations, including the American Red Cross and the Boy Scouts of America.

Ernest Hueter passed away on February 26, 2010, in Walnut Creek, California, and is survived by his wife Joan.

ESCAPE FROM NUREMBERG

JAMES KANAYA Veteran

"I ran as far as I could into the woods, and stayed where I was until dark. I stumbled into gun emplacements at night. I could hear Germans talking in their barracks."

Jimmie Kanaya, on his attempt as a prisoner to escape from the Germans, from an interview with *Veterans Chronicles*

He had spent the night in an air raid shelter beneath a Berlin railway station. It was Thanksgiving 1944. Overhead, the Allied bombing was nonstop, and to Second Lieutenant Jimmie Kanaya, the future seemed bleak. If the pummeling above didn't kill him, then the best he could look forward to was another POW camp, for he had been captured by the Germans two months prior and shipped off to Stuttgart.

His travels were just beginning, through, for the Germans wanted to make sure captured officers were imprisoned as far away from the western front as possible. Which was why Kanaya was in Berlin. He was being sent to Oflag 64 in Poland, a POW camp some 60 miles northwest of Warsaw, Poland. As he emerged into the sunshine the next morning, he was amazed by the thousands of men and boys with picks and shovels fixing the railroad tracks. "And yes, the trains were running on schedule."

The 442nd Regimental Combat Team, now considered the most decorated infantry regiment in U.S. Army history, was awarded eight Presidential Unit Citations with 21 of its soldiers later receiving the Medal of Honor.

With the Russians beginning their offensive in January 1945, Kanaya and his fellow POWs were forced to march 20 kilometers a day through snow and with temperatures dipping as low as 21 degrees below zero. "We were chased from the eastern front to the western front," reaching Hammelburg, Germany, two months later. Of the 1,400 POWs, only 400 survived the trek.

The next destination was Nuremburg. By then, Kanaya decided that he had enough and was determined to escape.

Kanaya joined the service at age 20 in the months prior to Pearl Harbor. A Nisei-American, he remained as committed to the war as anyone in the ranks of the

U.S., despite the mass relocation of Japanese-Americans—including his own family—to internment camps. Kanaya's father had been a farmer in Clackamas, Oregon, and later opened a fruit stand in downtown Portland. Dropping out of high school in his third year, Kanaya decided on a career in the military, and with his father's signature on the enlistment form, joined the Regular Army.

Halfway through basic training at Hamilton Field, California, Kanaya was sent to General Hospital in Santa Barbara, California, where he became classified as a medic, though as he would later recall, "I was commissioned in the Medical Administrative Corps." Kanaya explained, "My title was Battalion Surgeon Assistant, but I never had a day of medical training, just emergency first aid."

Assigned to the 3rd Battalion of the 442nd Regimental Combat Team, an all-Nisei outfit, Kanaya landed at Naples, Italy, in May 1944 and reached the front lines north of Rome about the same time that Allied forces were landing on the beaches of Normandy. Within weeks, the front lines had pushed across the border, and not long after Allied forces drove the Germans from the town of Bruyères, France, Kanaya was captured while assisting one of the battalions in evacuating casualties across the Vosges Mountains.

In April 1945, the war was winding down, and the Germans were desperate to relocate their prisoners where they couldn't be reached by either the Americans or the Russians. Once the decision was made to move the 8,000 to 10,000 Allied officers and enlisted men from Nuremburg, Kanaya saw his chance to escape. As the long column of prisoners moved out of the camp, U.S. planes began strafing the Germans, and Kanaya took off for the nearby woods during the confusion, running as fast and as far as he could. Finally, he found a crater in the woods, and crawled into it. He stayed there until after dark and then tried to find his way further away from the camp. "I stumbled into gun emplacements," he said. "I could hear Germans talking in their barracks. Good thing they didn't have dogs."

Close to dawn, Kanaya found himself across the road from the POW camp he had run away from, his stumbling around having gotten him closer to the prison than farther away. He wasn't getting anywhere, and it didn't make sense for him to continue trying to escape, so he walked to the main gate and turned himself in. Fortunately, within a few days, the camp was liberated by a tank battalion assigned to the 45th Division.

Colonel James K. Kanaya

At the end of the war, Kanaya went home. His parents had been allowed to leave the internment camp just before he left to go overseas, and were living in Chicago. After 30 days of R&R and eight weeks of schooling on the occupation of Japan (which he didn't need, since he wasn't sent there), Kanaya received a Regular Army commission and served in both Korea and Vietnam. He retired as a colonel in 1974 after 33 years of service.

Jimmie Kanaya resides with his wife Lynn in Gig Harbor, Washington.

SCALING THE CLIFFS AT POINTE DU HOC

LEONARD LOMELL Veteran

"We had to get the tremendous 155mm coastal guns that could fire ten to 12 miles out to sea and could fire on all of our invasion fleet lying there, thousands of ships."

Bud Lomell, on his mission to destroy the German guns at Pointe du Hoc, from an interview with *Veterans Chronicles*

D-Day, June 6, 1944. Pointe du Hoc was a sheer rock cliff that jutted out into the English Channel on the coast of Normandy, France. Located on the top of the heavily fortified cliff were the German army's largest coastal weapons, five 155mm guns capable of reaching Allied ships 25 kilometers out to sea, as well raining shells down on the tens of thousands of troops being ferried onto Omaha and Utah beaches. They had to be taken out of action.

Given the mission of scaling the cliffs and capturing the guns were three companies of the 2nd Battalion of the Army Rangers, D, E, and F. But first they had to get ashore. Sergeant Leonard "Bud" Lomell was the acting commander of D Company. "We had to run the gauntlet of 300 or 400 yards with the Germans firing at us with rifles, machine guns, anti-aircraft guns, and mortars, trying to blow us out of the water." Though wounded in his side, Lomell made it to the beach, and amid withering fire, the Rangers set about scaling the cliffs.

Following intense fighting, American soldiers rest at Pointe du Hoc, June 6, 1944.

The only way to reach the top was by climbing ropes, but how were they to get the ropes up there and secure them with the enemy waiting for them?

The cliffs of Pointe du Hoc and the beaches of Normandy were a far cry from Point Pleasant Beach, New Jersey, where Lomell grew up and where the major industry was fishing. Lomell and his friends would caddy at the local golf course all day, work the boardwalk at night, and go swimming in the Atlantic at midnight. "Then home for a sleep and start all over" the next day, he recalled in an interview with *Veterans Chronicles.*

Second Lieutenant Leonard G. Lomell

Lomell graduated from high school in 1937 and from college in 1941, "and in December of that year was Pearl Harbor." He ended up in Fort Dix, and from there, signed up for a new school, the first for Rangers. But instead of training recruits back at Fort Dix on Ranger tactics, which Lomell expected to be doing, he was promoted to first sergeant of the newly formed 2nd Ranger Battalion, and 15 months after Pearl Harbor, he was on a troop ship headed to England and eventually to the war in Europe... and the cliffs of Pointe du Hoc.

Fortunately for Lomell and the three companies staring up at the sheer cliff in front of them, the problem of getting ropes on top had been solved by British commandos. They would use small rockets capable of throwing the ropes with grapple hooks on the end high enough to clear the 100-foot cliffs. The Germans had other ideas, of course, lobbing rocks and grenades down on the men below and attempting to cut the ropes. "They were trying to drive us back into the sea, and we couldn't fight back climbing the ropes," Lomell recalled. Finally, the Allies managed to get men up there with a BAR,* which brushed the Germans back and allowed the others to climb the ropes.

According to Lomell, however, there was a major problem they hadn't expected: "There were no guns, as was told to us there would be." The Germans had moved them, replacing them with telephone poles to make it appear from the air that they were still there.

Finding them quickly was crucial to securing the beaches. Leapfrogging down a sunken road with fellow Ranger Sergeant Jack Kuhn, taking turns watching out for the enemy while looking over the hedgerows that lined the road, Lomell discovered the guns camouflaged in a field. Getting to them was difficult, as minutes before, German soldiers had passed by within 20 yards of the two Americans hiding in a ditch, but Lomell managed to disable them, eliminating the threat to the troops landing on Normandy.

Of the 200 Rangers sent to capture Pointe du Hoc, only 50 were capable of fighting at the end. Lomell was not one of them. "I was sent back because my wounds were infected with gangrene." He later fought at the Battle of Hürtgen Forest and the Battle of the Bulge, receiving a Distinguished Service Cross and a Silver Star, among other awards, and a promotion to second lieutenant.

After the war, Lomell returned to New Jersey, married Charlotte Ewart, and settled down on the coast at Tom's River, his wife's hometown. He received a degree from Rutgers University, passed the bar, and built a successful law practice.

Bud Lomell passed away on March 1, 2011, at age 91.

* BAR = Browning Automatic Rifle

ANGEL OF MOSUL

SUSAN LUZ Veteran

"I took care of the expectants—someone who was going to pass away. We had quite a few mass casualties. That would be Iraqi civilians, Iraqi soldiers, and yes, even terrorists."

Susan Luz, on one of her responsibilities as a nurse on being deployed to Iraq, from an interview with *Veterans Chronicles*

She had always known she wanted to be a military nurse and serve in Vietnam. After all, she was from a military family, her father having received the Silver Star for his heroism during World War II. The problem was, fighting his way through France and Germany, including the Battle of the Bulge, he knew too well the horrors of war, and it didn't help that he had seen the death of a nurse and was living with that image. He would not allow her to sign up. "That was it," she recalled. "The Irish dad said no."

So, instead, Luz (whose name was Corry before she was married) and her best friend and roommate at the University of Rhode Island decided to join the Peace Corps and were off to Brazil. At the time, the Peace Corps didn't assign teams of workers to the same locations, so her friend was sent to one village, while Luz went to another. There, she was brutally raped and beaten in broad daylight and left unconscious by the side of the road.

As in all wars, doctors and nurses have played a vital role on the battlefields in Iraq and Afghanistan. Pictured above, an Iraqi woman thanks American military personnel for saving the life of her son, who was injured by an insurgent blast.

She would be weeks in the hospital. Determined, however, to complete her mission, she stayed in Brazil during her recovery and later returned to her village. After finishing her assignment, she returned home to her family in Kingston, Rhode Island, where she was raised, and from there got her master's degree at Boston University in public health and community health nursing.

Luz then served a stint in Brazil with Project HOPE, and when she returned to the States, she worked for a while as an inner-city school nurse at Central High School in Providence, where she dealt with teenage pregnancy and served on programs enabling teen mothers to continue in school. Nights she worked at the Rhode Island Institute of Mental Health and later at Gateway Healthcare's Acute Residential Treatment Center.

Always in the back of her mind was the desire to be an Army nurse… so in 1983, at age 33, she told her father that she was planning to join the Army Reserves. Realizing her determination, he agreed not to stand in her way, and she was assigned to the 399th Combat Support Hospital, a Massachusetts reserve unit, where over the next 23 years, she slowly climbed the ranks to a full colonel, becoming the highest-ranking woman in the unit.

Then, in 2006, at age 56, Luz received a letter from the Department of the Army notifying her that her unit was being deployed to Iraq for 15 months. She was posted to a MASH-type unit in Mosul and within days after arriving, a mortar attack severely wounded a fellow nurse and brought in mass casualties.

As a public health nurse with certification as a psychiatric nurse, Luz's role in Iraq was that of helping service members heal from emotional trauma and providing comfort to dying soldiers. There was a lot of the latter, for while she was in Iraq, there would be 13 more MASCALs (incidents of mass casualties), and in between, hundreds of soldiers who needed counseling.

When she broke her arm, Luz refused to be sent to Riyadh in Saudi Arabia to recuperate, although she would be eight weeks in a cast. "I needed to be with my soldiers," she said.

"I was the morale officer," she indicated in her interview with *Veterans Chronicles*. "A cookout, a movie night—we brought ourselves together. We were a family." She even opened a beauty salon to help maintain the morale of the women on the base. But she was much more than that. "Back then, PTSD [Post Traumatic Stress Disorder]… no one wanted to talk about it. Now the Army, the veterans' hospitals, have really pushed the need for soldiers coming back who have problems to really talk about it."

It was a condition that Luz recognized early on due to her education and training. She pointed out that soldiers are supposed to be brave; they internalize their anger because they always have to be on guard in the war zone. When they come home, "they can't get it out of their system."

Colonel Susan P. Luz

During the time she was in Iraq, Luz's unit treated more than 30,000 wounded and endured 300 mortar attacks at Mosul and at Al Asad, where it relocated and established a Level I hospital during the military's ramp-up of forces in 2007. As she indicated in a book she wrote on her experiences in the war, "I don't dwell on it, but I can't forget the injuries we saw. The faces. The lives. The people."

In May 2010, Susan Luz retired from the Army. She and her husband George currently reside in North Scituate, Rhode Island.

SHOOTING DOWN THE ENEMY, AND BEING SHOT DOWN

WALKER MAHURIN Veteran

"I had the luck to become involved with an underground outfit that had spies, and they had been in contact with the Royal Air Force through the BBC."

Bud Mahurin, on being forced to bail out over France after shooting down a German bomber, from an interview with *Veterans Chronicles*

Below him, the Dormier Do-217 exploded into a ball of flame. Which didn't happen any too soon, for Major Walker "Bud" Mahurin's P-47 Thunderbolt was hit as well, smoke pouring from the engine. The German bomber had been running for safety over the treetops with Mauhrin on its tail. In the throes of going down, however, the bomber's dorsal gunner had managed to hit the P-47 with sufficient rounds for Mahurin to know that he couldn't keep it in the air.

Though he was a little low at 200 feet, Mahurin opened the canopy and safely parachuted into an open field. Overhead in the noontime sky, as Mahurin once recalled in an interview with a newspaper, fellow fighter pilots circled like bees around a beehive.

The P-47 Thunderbolt fighter-bomber, flown by Bud Mahurin to become one of America's top "ace" pilots.

With this part of central France still in the hands of the Germans, Mahurin unhooked his harness and took off across the field as fast as he could. As the Germans were certain to be looking for him, he ran for miles before he fell, exhausted, into a ditch. He had to find a safe place to hide until he could figure out what to do next. Nearby in a field was haystack, and he figured it was as good a place as any to avoid being found by enemy soldiers searching for the owner of the parachute.

For Mahurin, shooting down German planes was almost routine, but being shot down on March 27, 1944, was not. He was already a "double-ace" (ten victories) at the time, including such kills as two Fw-190s during the Schweinfurt-Regensburg raid in August 1943, three Messerschmitt Bf-110s over Bremen in October, and three more Bf-110s over Oldenburg in November. He accounted for five more enemy aircraft shot down during that winter, and in March

1944, as he escorted bombers over Berlin, the Luftwaffe launched 400 fighters, and Mahurin shot down three Fw-190s and a Junkers bomber.

Mahurin attributed his interest in flying to the exploits of Charles Lindbergh, when he flew across the Atlantic. "That made a lot of difference in my life." Born in Benton Harbor, Michigan, Mahurin studied engineering at Purdue University, but then left and joined the Civilian Pilot Training Program (CPTP). Trained at Chickasha, Oklahoma, which was an official military ground school, he graduated in April 1942.

When Mahurin finished the CPT Program, he was automatically an aviation cadet. From Chickasha, he received further training at Randolph Air Force Base in Texas, then went on to an advanced flying school at Ellington Field near Houston, and finally to Fort Dix, New Jersey, where he was assigned to the 63rd Squadron of the 56th Fighter Group. Stationed for a time at Mitchell Field, Long Island, Mahurin's squadron flew an early model of the P-47 known as a "razorback."

Mahurin flew missions for 17 months out of England before getting shot down over France. How he managed to escape from the haystack and into the hands of the French underground is unclear, but his plight was certainly known to his fellow pilots circling in the sky above and would have been reported. In any case, 27 days passed before the RAF* was able to fly him out to safety.

There was a problem, though; Mahurin's flying days were over in Europe. Having been with the French Resistance, he knew too much, and had he been shot down again and captured by the Germans, the Luftwaffe would have treated him as a spy. So he was sent home, and got himself assigned to the 3rd Air Commando Group, flying missions in the Pacific in a P-51. Promoted to lieutenant colonel, he downed a Japanese bomber in January 1945 in his last action of World War II.

Mahurin's military flying career, however, was not yet over, as he was trained to fly the F-86 Sabre jet in Korea. Matched in dogfights against the Russian-built MiG-15s, he managed to shoot down three of the enemy before being downed by North Korean ground fire while strafing a truck. Crash-landing and breaking his arm, he was captured and spent 16 months in a North Korean prison, where he was subjected to intense questioning and harsh treatment. He was finally released in September 1953 and was promoted to colonel.

Colonel Walker M. Mahurin

With a total of 24.25 planes destroyed in combat, he was the only American pilot to shoot down enemy aircraft in two theaters (Europe and the Pacific) and in two wars.

Walker Mahurin retired from military service in 1956 and went to work in the aerospace industry. He passed away on May 11, 2010, at his home in Newport Beach, California, leaving behind his wife Joan.

* RAF = Royal Air Force

ASSAULT ON AN ANTHILL

WALTER JOSEPH MARM Veteran

"I told my men to hold their fire, not to shoot me up, and I ran across about 30 meters of open terrain, and got to the base of that anthill, and then threw the grenade over the top."

Joe Marm, on charging the enemy while attempting to rescue a platoon surrounded by North Vietnamese, from an interview with *Veterans Chronicles*

November 14, 1965. It looked like a giant anthill, and it was—six or so feet high, solidified, and surrounded by trees and shrubs. Ants weren't the problem, though. Instead, it was the intense fire of the North Vietnamese soldiers behind the hill. The obstacle had to be cleared out, and soon, as casualties for Alpha Company were rising. Grabbing an LAW (light anti-tank weapon)—a bazooka-type weapon—platoon leader First Lieutenant Walter Joseph Marm fired into the hill and was greeted with yelling and screaming from the other side.

Unfortunately, it wasn't enough, for the hill wasn't blown apart and the enemy quickly regrouped and began firing again from behind it. At that point, Marm told his men to hold their fire as they might shoot him in the back, and disregarding the bullets whizzing around him, he raced across the open terrain with his M-16. Reaching the base of the anthill, he threw a grenade over the top of the mound, and when it went off, he charged around the hill to finish the job by shooting the few North Vietnamese still alive.

Marm and his platoon were part of the sweep through the Ia Drang Valley near Chu Pong Mountain in the Central Highlands of Vietnam by the 1st Battalion of the 7th Cavalry in the 1st Cavalry Division (Airmobile).* Earlier in the day, Bravo Company had come under attack by hundreds of North

Transport helicopters land infantrymen at LZ X-Ray during the Battle of Ia Drang. The Battle of Ia Drang was the first major engagement between the regular forces of the United States and North Vietnamese.

* The Airmobile unit was a new battlefield strategy being tried out by the Army in which helicopters, previously used exclusively to evacuate wounded soldiers and transport supplies, would be employed as well to deploy troops to fronts and behind the lines.

Vietnamese in what has become known as the Battle of Ia Drang. It was the first major encounter between U.S. troops and North Vietnamese Army (NVA) regulars.

For the 2nd Platoon of Bravo Company, pursuing the enemy on the right flank, the situation disintegrated rapidly as the NVA attack intensified and the platoon became cut off from the rest of the company and trapped. Unable to fight its way through, the platoon formed a defensive perimeter to blunt the waves of attacks and hold on until help arrived.

As getting through to the 2nd Platoon was going to be difficult, Marm's platoon was attached to Bravo Company to help strengthen it for the rescue effort.

The first attempt at 4:00 in the afternoon had failed. With his platoon now leading the second effort, and having taken out the anthill, Marm motioned to his men that it was safe to cross the clearing. He was wrong. Suddenly, a shot rang out, and he was hit by a bullet which shattered his jaw. Exiting from his neck, the bullet missed his jugular vein by an inch.

Marm, the son of a state trooper, was born and raised in Washington, Pennsylvania, and after high school attended Duquesne University, where he studied finance. With the U.S. heading to war in Southeast Asia, after graduating from college, Marm decided to enlist in the Army. Following basic and advanced training at Fort Gordon, Georgia, and six months in Officer Candidate School (OCS), he then trained as a Ranger.

The Army needed junior infantry officers, however. As Marm recalled, nearing the end of Ranger School, he was told, "Your orders are now being changed. You're allowed one phone call home tonight to tell your family and friends you won't be going to your original destination." He was then off to Fort Benning, Georgia, where he was assigned to the 7th Cavalry.

By September 1965, Marm was in Vietnam.

As Marm fell to the ground, he recovered enough to make sure his jaw was still there. As he later said in an interview, he didn't know if he still had the bottom part of his mouth. He did. Fortunately, a medic showed up at his side and he was patched up and evacuated back to the battalion command post.

On the battlefront, the 2nd Platoon of Bravo Company managed to survive three attacks by the NVA during the night. The platoon's chain

Colonel Walter J. Marm

of command being wiped out, a buck sergeant took charge of the unit, and throughout the night called for mortar and artillery fire on North Vietnamese positions whenever he heard a noise. The next day, the platoon was rescued.

Following months of recuperation at Valley Forge Army Hospital in Pennsylvania, where his jaw was wired shut and he lived on baby food, Marm continued his career in the Army, including a repeat tour in Vietnam. After 30 years of service, Marm retired as a colonel in 1995.

Joe Marm and his wife Deborah reside in Fremont, North Carolina, where they raise pigs.

ATTACK ON LA FIÈRE MANOR

JOHN MARR Veteran

"It's been argued when airborne types get together whether we would have done better if we had dropped with solidarity and gathered in large battalions, or were we more effective scattered out as we were."

John Marr, on parachuting near Ste-Mère-Église during the early morning hours of D-Day and the costly battle for the bridge at La Fière, from an interview with *Veterans Chronicles*

Normally, the Merderet River was not much more than a meandering creek. On June 6, 1944, it was anything but, having been converted by the Germans into a huge shallow lake by opening locks at Carentan at high tide and flooding the fields around the La Fière causeway leading from Ste-Mère-Église to Cauquigny, France.

Unfortunately, for Second Lieutenant John Marr, he experienced firsthand the cold water of the flooded fields. Jumping into Normandy on June 6, 1944, with other paratroopers of the 507th Parachute Infantry Regiment in the 82nd Airborne, Marr found himself up to his armpits in water before he managed to pull himself up onto a railroad embankment, where he joined others of the 82nd taking refuge there.

Of particular importance to the 82nd Airborne Division was the bridge across Merderet near the farm known as Manoir de La Fière, a grouping of stone buildings a couple of miles west of Ste-Mère-Église. Here was one of only two locations where the river could be crossed by armor. For the Allied forces to be successful, crossing the Merderet and holding the bridges and causeway would be crucial to moving inland. Plus, the 82nd was scattered on both sides of the river and had to be brought together. On the other hand, if the Germans were going to stop the invasion, this was the place to do it.

The battle for the La Fière bridge raged for four days, and it was both bloody and costly to both sides. What with the frontal assaults, counterattacks, and incessant shelling by mortars and tanks, dead and wounded soldiers were strewn

Paratroopers of the 82nd Airborne Division prepare to board their transport plane to Holland during Operation Market Garden, September 17, 1944.

along the causeway and at both ends of the bridge. The causeway had become a gauntlet of destruction.

Marr was born on a farm in Warrensburg, Missouri, and by the age of ten, he was driving four horses behind a two-gang plow. When the farm failed to produce enough to earn a living, Marr and his brother followed their father into mining, for which the boys each got one dollar a day. "We were going to high school at the time, so we would drop out except for the winter quarter. So it took both of us six years to get through high school."

Marr was drafted into the Army in June 1941, the first of six brothers to serve in the war, four in overseas combat. After basic training at Camp Roberts, California, he was encouraged into joining the paratroopers by the commander of the 506th Parachute Infantry Regiment, and was sent to Fort Benning, Georgia, where "we learned how to use dynamite and TNT and all kinds of stuff to blow everything up."

Then came Pearl Harbor. Sent to Salt Lake City Army Airfield, Marr received training on how to ski, maneuver over passes, and sleep out in -35 degree weather. Whatever the military had in mind for him at that time, however, it was not to be, for he was soon back at Fort Benning. After attending Officer Candidate School (OCS) and coming out as a second lieutenant, he was deployed to Europe as a member of Company G in the 507th Regiment.

As he looked across the hotly contested causeway at La Fière, Marr was glad in a way that the 82nd hadn't been dropped as a unified force into Normandy. Despite their badly missing the drop zones, there was an advantage in being scattered around the landscape, namely the fact that units of the 82nd could come at the Germans from different directions, keeping them off balance. Now, because there were men on both sides of the bridge—in front, behind, and to the flanks of the enemy—as Marr put it, the "small groups could create a lot of mischief."

Finally, on June 9, 1944, after the four days of ferocious fighting, the tide of the battle turned in favor of the Allies, and the Germans began to pull back from Cauquigny, leaving the causeway at La Fière in the hands of the 82nd.

After the battle, Marr was put in command of Company B of the 507th during the Battle of the Bulge. The company was then detached from the 82nd and assigned to the 17th Airborne as a reserve unit,

Colonel John W. Marr

Marr later jumping into Germany in Operation Varsity, a joint American and British airborne operation to secure a foothold across the Rhine River by capturing bridges and towns in northern Germany.

John Marr remained in the Army, earning his Army aviator wings, and was promoted to commander of the 17th Combat Aviation Group in Vietnam. He retired from the service in January 1974. He and his wife Willa reside in Alexandria, Virginia.

TERRORISTS IN AL TARMIA

MARCO MARTINEZ Veteran

"As soon as we got into the area, you felt there's a weird electricity in the air. Your sixth sense went off, and you felt that something was not right. Upon doing the reconnaissance, all hell broke loose."

Marco Martinez, on being ambushed by Fadayeen terrorists while patrolling in the Baghdad suburb of Al Tarmia, from an interview with *Veterans Chronicles*

April 12, 2003. His fire team squad leader had his leg almost blown off by a grenade. So Corporal Marco Martinez of Company G in the 2nd Battalion of the 5th Marines, 1st Marine Division did what he had to do… he took over. They had gotten intelligence that a terrorist force of Fadayeen militants was massing in the town of Al Tarmia, a suburb about 12 miles north of Baghdad. According to Martinez, "Upon doing the reconnaissance, all hell broke loose. RPGs [rocket-propelled grenades] went off. Guys started popping out of windows." In short, they were in the middle of an ambush.

Bullets were pinging off the vehicles—one of which was hit by mortars and lost right away—and the air was thick with the smell of smoke and burnt gunpowder. "Initially, we took two wounded right off the bat."

On April 9, 2003, Baghdad fell to coalition forces as Iraqis joined American forces in tearing down the statue of Saddam Hussein in Firdos Square.

For four hours, the fighting was from house to house. "No matter where you were at, where you were stepping, there was someone shooting at you." Minutes later, Martinez's squad leader went down, and he took over. After fighting its way through a building and into a courtyard, the squad found itself pinned down by heavy small arms fire from inside a house facing the courtyard, and was forced to take shelter behind palm trees. Within minutes, a Marine took a hit and collapsed on the ground, alive but paralyzed by a bullet in his spine.

Glancing to his right, Martinez noticed an RPG lying on the ground that had belonged to a terrorist killed earlier. He picked it up, figured out how to shoot it, and pumped a grenade into the house, stunning those inside, which gave the Marines enough time to evacuate the wounded soldier. Shortly afterwards, as enemy fire resumed and grew even more intense, Martinez knew that something had to be done or they were all going to be picked off.

So he charged the house.

For Martinez, the path to becoming a Marine had been strewn with obstacles. For though his father had been a career Army Ranger and Martinez had been raised around military bases, such as Kirkland Air Force Base in Albuquerque, New Mexico, and Fort Bliss in El Paso, Texas, he also grew up on the streets of Las Cruces, New Mexico. Then a Marine recruiter walked down the hallway at his school and he knew immediately what he wanted to do with his life. The following week, Martinez showed up at the local Marine recruiting station.

But getting into the Marines was not going to be that easy. The recruiter warned him that he was going to have trouble enlisting because of the tattoo on his back. "Anytime you go into the military, they want to know every single thing about you. They want to see any markings, scars, anything like that; they screen those out right away, because a lot of times, tattoos have meanings that other people may not know about."

The next step was the Marine Entrance Processing Station (MEPS), and the gunnery sergeant there was reluctant to let him in the Corps, but somehow Martinez was able to convince the sergeant how much being a Marine meant to him and how he wanted to make his parents proud. He was sent to MCRD San Diego for boot camp and received additional training at the School of Infantry at Camp Pendleton, California.

When 9/11 occurred, Martinez was stationed in Okinawa, Japan. Like most men in the ranks at the time, he couldn't wait to help settle the score with the terrorists. He and the men in his unit were "like a pit bull on a leash." The problem was the AO (Area of Operations) for the 5th Marines was the Pacific, so the 1st Marines went first, and "we were held back." It was February 2003 before Martinez and his battalion were deployed to Iraq as part of Operation Iraqi Freedom.

Charging across the courtyard, Martinez was alone. All he could think was that he had to clear the house of the enemy. When he got close enough, he "prepped a hand grenade and threw it in the window." Entering quickly, he wiped out the four terrorists inside. More than 75 of the Fadayeen fighters were killed during the raid on Al Tarmia that day. Fortunately, Martinez made it through unscathed.

Sergeant Marco A. Martinez

After the war, Marco Martinez settled down in Dana Point, California, where he worked full-time in nuclear security while studying for his business degree at San Diego State University. Recently, he returned from a yearlong study abroad program in South Korea, where he graduated with honors.

SPIGOT MORTARS OVER RIDGE 352

DONALD MATES Veteran

"At midnight, out came the Japanese. We called them 'roving wolves'... they ran all over the place. They were absolutely fearless, and they came right at you."

Don Mates, on a fierce nighttime battle for a ridge on Iwo Jima, from an interview with *Veterans Chronicles*

The spigot mortars tumbled in the air and you couldn't tell where they were coming from... except for the trail of sparks. Which is why the patrol was sent out at night. They had to be located, for they were blowing huge holes in the volcanic sand of Iwo Jima, and casualties were mounting in the 3rd Marine Division. Volunteering for the mission was Private Donald Mates, along with seven others in the 3rd Reconnaissance Battalion.

To find out where the mortars were concealed, the patrol climbed Hill 352 and dug in for the night, two men in foxholes near the top, two 25 feet down the hill, two more—Mates and baseball player Jimmy Trimble—25 feet further down, and finally, the remaining two below them. It was eerily quiet. What they didn't know was that the Japanese were gathering on the other side of the ridge. Just after midnight on March 1, 1945, a flare suddenly lit the sky... and all hell broke loose.

The Battle of Iwo Jima saw some of the fiercest fighting in the Pacific in World War II. It was the only Marine Corps battle that saw more American casualties than Japanese. Of the 22,000 Japanese defenders on Iwo Jima, only 216 were taken prisoner—the rest were killed, missing, or presumed dead.

"They came right at you," Mates recalled. "They were absolutely fearless." Noise and confusion reigned, as the enemy swarmed toward the platoon. "For about two and a half hours, it was a real tough battle."

The enemy wore phosphorous pins on the back of their collars, which would glow in the starlight and flares. That way, their officers behind them would know where they were and direct them to the left or right. "When I turned around, I could see the phosphorous," Mates indicated, which meant he was seeing soldiers who had already gone by him. The men higher on the hill, as he found out later, were either dead or severely wounded, and Trimble, in the foxhole with him, had been wounded in the right shoulder by a bayonet.

The enemy was close enough to Mates that he could hear the "click, click" of grenades being struck together, which is how the Japanese ignited them, either by hitting them on their helmet or smacking them together. They had no pins to pull. Within seconds, two of the grenades came flying into the foxhole, one landing behind Trimble, who tried to turn away from it, and the another dropping between Mates' legs.

There was no time to react. Both grenades exploded.

Mates was raised in Cleveland, Ohio, and was talked into joining the Marines at age 17 by a recruiter who came to the high school and promised him he could finish school if he enlisted. He would need his parent's signature, since he wasn't 18, which he got. "P.S., I didn't finish high school. They nailed me right away." But they credited basic training for his last semester in school, so he was able to graduate after boot camp.

He was sent to Paris Island, South Carolina, and was offered the opportunity to join combat intelligence. It sounded better to him than firing a machine gun or a mortar. Little did he know that he'd be lugging an M1 rifle in the middle of some of the toughest fighting in the South Pacific.

From Paris Island, it was on to Camp Lejeune, North Carolina, for eight weeks of combat training and eight weeks of intelligence school, one week of radio school, and one week of demolition school. Finally, he found himself on a troop ship to Norfolk, Virginia, and from there, he was sent to Guam on an aircraft carrier, where he was involved in patrolling and setting up ambushes, and in intelligence reporting to G2.

In February 1945, a couple of months after the last of the Japanese were being rooted out of the jungles of Guam, Mates and the others in his battalion boarded ship for Iwo Jima.

The explosion in the foxhole that night broke both of Mates' legs and blew away flesh on his thighs and legs. The blast had also peppered the back, upper arms, and head of Trimble with shrapnel. Somehow, Mates managed to crawl out of the hole, and as he reached in to help his partner, a Japanese soldier with a grenade strapped to him jumped into the hole and wrapped himself around Trimble. "The bottom half of [him] just evaporated."

Private Donald A. Mates

Screeching for help and yelling the passwords, Mates was rescued by the two men from the foxhole below them—Privates James White and Lee Blanchard—who bandaged him up and managed to hold off the enemy until reinforcements drove the Japanese back into the jungle.

Mates spent 16 months recovering in hospitals, suffering through treatments for gangrene. After the war, he attended Arizona State, graduating in 1951, and worked in the financial industry before retiring.

Donald Mates and his wife Mary reside in Palm Beach, Florida.

FROM THE BRIG TO THE BATTLEFIELD

JAKE MCNIECE Veteran

"One thousand C-47s loaded with supplies were circling over France to see if I could get a signal to them that they could guide in on through this inclement weather."

Jake McNiece, on signaling with secret equipment after parachuting into the besieged city of Bastogne, Belgium, from an interview with *Veterans Chronicles*

Saturday, December 23, 1944. The city of Bastogne, Belgium, was covered with a heavy blanket of snow, and it was bitter cold. The night before, the temperature had dropped to -22 degrees with a blowing mixture of snow and sleet. Thus far, the perimeter around Bastogne had held, but for how long was uncertain, for the city had been completely surrounded by four reinforced divisions of the German Army, including two divisions of Panzers.

Though a portion of the Panzer force moved on, all seven of the highways and the three rail lines in and out of Bastogne were cut and controlled by the enemy. Capturing Bastogne was essential to the German drive through the Ardennes at the height of what became known as the Battle of the Bulge.

Parachuting into the middle of the city on the 23rd was Private Jake McNiece with a handful of men. In an interview with *Veterans Chronicles*, McNiece recalled that the situation in Bastogne was getting desperate. "They were out of medicine, down to ten rounds of ammunition per gun. They had little food. They didn't have proper clothing for the weather." The only way to relieve the situation was to drop the supplies by air, but the weather had been so bad, drop areas could not be seen, and airlifts were considered impossible.

On this mission, McNiece was in charge of a specially trained group of battle-hardened paratroopers, known as "Pathfinders," used in high-risk situations to mark landing and drop zones behind enemy lines. McNiece knew he was pushing his luck, for few Pathfinders survived more than a jump or two. This would be his third.

The Pathfinders were the first Americans in Normandy on D-Day, dropping behind enemy lines to help prepare the drop zones for the 82nd and 101st Airborne divisions later that morning.

Private Jake E. McNiece

McNiece was the first to admit that his military service had been rocky. Heroic actions during combat were matched by antics that led to his being demoted and confined to a stockade. Insubordination, unauthorized leaves, and drunken brawls often landed him in the brig. Yet, when his bravery, skill, and ferocious fighting ability were needed on the front lines, he was released. Invariably, he'd end up back in the stockade again.

McNiece was raised in the small community of Maysville, Oklahoma. "We were farm folk, and we grew up in the Depression, dust storms in the late '20s, and then off to war." At age 23, he enlisted on September 2, 1942, and trained with the 506th Parachute Infantry Regiment, which was ultimately incorporated into the 101st Airborne Division. "I soldiered well, but I used all the rest of the time for my enjoyment," he confessed. "I didn't go for the malarkey of saluting officers, or shining shoes, and shaving."

Assigned to the 1st Battalion, a demolition unit charged with blowing up bridges, McNiece saw more than his share of action during the Normandy campaign, but nothing was more challenging than jumping into the fog and severe winter weather enveloping the city of Bastogne. There were no signal lights, no flares, nothing on the ground to mark a landing spot. He and his men were thus facing the prospect of either being shot by the Germans during the jump or dropping into the middle of the enemy surrounding the city. He knew he had to do it, though, for the American forces inside Bastogne were his own 101st Airborne.

At 6:45 a.m. on the 23rd, two planes, each carrying half of the 20 Pathfinders, took off.

As they neared Bastogne, the aircraft began to be fired on by the German forces. With no other way of defending themselves, McNiece's pilot dropped down to treetop level to scatter the Germans. At that point, McNiece noticed a large cemetery, which could only mean they were over Bastogne. The plane pulled back to parachute jump altitude; McNiece and his men bailed out. Landing in a field just outside the town, they immediately sent up an orange smoke signal to guide the second plane in.

McNiece quickly set up special transmitting equipment—Eureka beacons—for sending a signal to the C-47s loaded with supplies circling above. The signal picked up by receiving equipment on the C-47s identified the drop zone, and before noon that morning, hundreds of brightly colored parachutes filled the skies. As the bundles hit the ground, a task force of soldiers rushed from the city to drag in the desperately needed ammunition, food, and medical supplies, as well as winter clothing.

After the war, Jake McNiece returned to the States and eventually settled in Ponca City, Oklahoma, where he went to work for the post office. A widower, he married his second wife Martha, who made him give up the drinking and brawling as a condition of marrying him. And he did. They have been married for almost 60 years.

ATTACK ON LZ X-RAY

HAROLD MOORE, JR. Veteran

"My battle was six miles east of Cambodia. We defeated the enemy after three days, and he fell back, leaving hundreds of his dead on the field. He fell back with his survivors and wounded into Cambodia. We wanted to pursue him to the death."

Hal Moore, on the Battle of Ia Drang Valley and his being stopped on the border from pursuing the North Vietnamese Army (NVA), from an interview with *Veterans Chronicles*

November 16, 1965. The battle had raged for two days and nights south of the Drang River and northwest of Plei Me in the central highlands of South Vietnam. The assault by the North Vietnamese Army (NVA) against the 1st Battalion of the 7th Cavalry Regiment in the 1st Cavalry Division was finally repulsed. Despite being heavily outnumbered, the 1st Battalion, commanded by Lieutenant General Hal Moore, had managed to stem the onslaught of North Vietnamese streaming out of the trees, rescue one of its platoons that had been "lost" (cut off and surrounded by the enemy), and prevent its landing zone (LZ X-Ray) from being overrun.

Using Huey helicopters, the 1st Battalion of the 7th Cavalry, as well as other elements of the 7th and 5th Cavalry, had been shuttled into the highlands on a reconnaissance mission to track down an NVA force that had attacked a U.S. Army Special Forces base at Plei Me.

Moore's plan on the landing of his rifle companies at LZ X-Ray was to move two of his companies (Alpha and elements of Bravo) northwest past a creek bed, while the third company (Charlie) was to head south toward Chu Pong Mountain. Delta, Moore's heavy weapons company comprised of mortars and machine gun units, was held in reserve, while most of Bravo was kept near the center of the LZ as a strike force.

Before long, the 1st Battalion came under intense fire on all fronts and was in extreme danger of being wiped out. Despite the repeated assaults by the enemy, it managed to establish and secure a 360-degree

Hal Moore inspects enemy casualties at LZ X-Ray. After Moore's 1/7 Cavalry repulsed the NVA following intense fighting from November 14 to 16, 1965, the North Vietnamese would attack and overrun a marching column from the 2/7 Cavalry on November 17, the most deadly ambush of U.S. forces during the war.

perimeter, helped by air strikes and artillery. In the process, hundreds of North Vietnamese were cut down by rifle and machine gun fire and by grenades as they charged in waves, reaching to within yards of the battalion's positions. Finally, after the two days of intense fighting on multiple fronts, the NVA forces began to withdraw into Cambodia, leaving the bodies of hundreds of their soldiers strewn over the battleground.

Moore's battalion had managed to survive, but whatever satisfaction he must have felt had to have been tempered by the heavy losses taken by the battalion (79 killed and 121 wounded out of about 450 men).* Not being able to pursue the enemy was also troubling. "I was taught at West Point, when you defeat an enemy on the battlefield," he recalled, "you pursue that enemy to death." Moore, however, was ordered to stop at the Cambodian border.

Born in rural Bardstown, Kentucky, Moore had long wanted to go to West Point, but it took moving to Washington, DC, where he graduated from high school and attended George Washington University for two years, before he managed to secure an appointment from a Georgia congressman. His persistence had paid off.

Graduating from West Point in 1945 and commissioned a second lieutenant, Moore served with the 187th Airborne Infantry Division in Japan during the occupation from 1945 to 1948, at which time he was reassigned to the 82nd Airborne Division, where he volunteered to join the Airborne Test Section, testing experimental parachutes.

In Korea, Moore was a captain in the 17th Infantry Regiment of the 7th Infantry Division. He commanded both a rifle company and a heavy mortar company in combat. Afterward, he served at West Point for three years as an instructor in infantry tactics and in other positions with the Command and General Staff College and the National War College while earning a master's degree in international relations from Harvard University.

In 1964 at Fort Benning, Georgia, he was assigned command of a battalion in the 11th Air Assault Division undergoing air assault and air mobility training. In July 1965, the division was re-designated as the 1st Cavalry Division, and Moore's battalion ended up with him in Vietnam and at Ia Drang.

* The 2nd Battalion of the 7th Cavalry and the 2nd Battalion of the 5th Cavalry, which had also been shuttled in by Hueys, was ambushed the next day near LZ Albany during a tactical march toward Chu Pon Mountain. The attack was the most deadly ambush of a U.S. unit during the course of the entire war.

Lieutenant General Harold G. Moore, Jr.

After Vietnam, Moore served as an assistant chief of staff with the 8th Army in South Korea and as commanding general of the 7th Infantry Division, before rotating back to the U.S. as commanding general of the Army Training Center at Fort Ord, California. His last assignment was as deputy chief of staff for personnel for the Department of the Army.

Hal Moore retired in 1977 and became executive president of the Crested Butte Ski Area in Colorado. He resides today in Auburn, Alabama.

THE MAKING OF AN ADMIRAL

THOMAS MOORER Veteran

"My mission was to find those carriers, which I did. I ran right into a big flight of planes, a couple hundred from the same carriers that attacked Pearl Harbor. I was alone."

Thomas Moorer, on the tracking down of Japanese carriers headed for Wake Island, from an interview with *Veterans Chronicles*

February 19, 1942. He was looking for the Japanese carriers headed for Wake Island. And he found them. The problem was that he had also run smack into a couple of hundred enemy planes… and he was alone.

Lieutenant Thomas Moorer, flight officer of Squadron VP-22 out of Pearl Harbor, was clearly in enemy territory, for the Japanese had already taken Guam, landed in the Philippines and Borneo, and captured Wake Island. With the Japanese on the move toward the Dutch East Indies (today, Indonesia), Moorer's mission was simply to find out where the enemy was and where it was going.

Thomas Moorer would have a first-hand view of the devastation caused at Pearl Harbor before going to serve with distinction throughout World War II, eventually becoming chairman of the Joint Chiefs of Staff.

Bumping into the Japanese Zeros was more than he counted on, and the encounter ended badly after nine of the Zeros broke off from the formation. It wasn't long before his PBY-5 Catalina was hit and in trouble. "They were firing incendiary bullets," Moorer recalled. "They were low velocity; I could actually see the bullets." With the PBY on fire and headed down, the Zeros rejoined their formation.

Fortunately—at least it seemed so at the time—he was seen by a Philippine ship that rescued him and his seven-man crew from the water. Unfortunately, it was an ammunition ship. "I told my crew to get back on the stern, that we were going to get attacked again." If that happened, the men were supposed to jump overboard. Before long, Japanese dive bombers found the ship, blew the bow off, and sunk it, but as the stern continued to float, Moorer and a couple of his crew managed to crawl back on it and cut two of the lifeboats loose.

Then the Japanese returned.

Moorer was born in Mount Willing, a small community south of Montgomery, Alabama. After attending high school in Montgomery, he decided he wanted a career in the Navy, and was granted an appointment to the U.S. Naval Academy. Moorer's first assignment was the cruiser USS *Salt Lake City*, and from there, he found himself serving in the gunnery and engineering departments of the USS *New Orleans*.

When he decided he wanted to fly, Moorer was accepted by the United States Naval Aviation Training School at Pensacola, Florida. His first assignment as a naval aviator was to Fighting Squadron 1-B aboard the USS *Langley*, the nation's first aircraft carrier. Subsequent duties and squadron transfers included the USS *Lexington* and the USS *Enterprise*, where he joined Patrol Squadron 22 and learned to fly the PBY Catalina flying patrol boats.

With Patrol Squadron 22 transferred to Fleet Air Wing 10, on December 7, 1941, Moorer was stationed at Pearl Harbor. "I saw the Japanese planes from a distance. They came in three ways: east side, west side, and through the saddle." They began by strafing the American fighters on the ground. Moorer managed to get one of the planes in the air, but by then, the Japanese had gone north.

Now, two months later, he was again looking up, helpless as the enemy fighters strafed the lifeboats, forcing them to jump back into the water. The situation was bleak. No potable water. No compass. But they did have sails, and Moorer, though wounded, managed to get them to uninhabited Bathurst Island off the north coast of Australia. An SOS drawn in the sand was seen by a reconnaissance plane, and Moorer and his crew were soon picked up by an Australian freighter. Despite horizontal bombing by the Japanese, they made it to Darwin, Australia, and relative safety.

After serving with Patrol Squadron 101 for a few months, Moorer returned to the United States, but was soon sent to England at the request of Admiral Earnest King on an assignment dealing with mines being laid on the bottom of the sea by the Germans.

Back in the U.S., he spent six weeks with the 5th Bomber Command, and in March 1944, he became the gunnery and tactical officer on the staff of the commander of the Naval Air Forces in the Atlantic.

Admiral Thomas H. Moorer (right)

Moorer continued to have a distinguished career in the service, having been promoted to vice admiral in 1962 and admiral in 1964. He served both as commander-in-chief of the Pacific Fleet and of the Atlantic Fleet, the first Naval officer to have done so. He was chief of Naval Operations from 1967 to 1970 and chairman of the Joint Chiefs of Staff from 1970 until 1974.

Thomas Moorer passed away on February 5, 2004, at the U.S. Naval Hospital in Bethesda, Maryland. His wife Carrie passed away on March 22, 2007.

THE WAR BEGAN HERE –
JUNE 25, 1950
38TH PARALLEL
COURTESY
1ST CAVALRY DIVISION

BAGGING THREE BETTYS

JAMES MOREHEAD Veteran

"We had terrible losses. In one of our first battles, seven P-40s went up against the Zeros, and seven P-40s didn't come back."

Jim Morehead, on the defense of Java during the early days of the war, from an interview with *Veterans Chronicles*

They had bombed the port of Darwin, Australia, and were on their way home. For some reason, the 31 Japanese Bettys—the name given to the medium-range G4M bombers by Allied pilots—were flying well below their normal cruising altitude of 30,000 feet and were seemingly oblivious to the fighters closing in on them. James Morehead recalled it as the "first time I'd ever seen them at a comfortable altitude," and thought, "Man, we ought to take advantage of this."

As Morehead indicated in his interview with *Veterans Chronicles*, in escorting a bomber, a fighter plane has got to weave back and forth around the bomber because it is faster. In this case, the Japanese fighters had swung away from the bombers. Morehead pointed out that at this stage of the war, all was going well for the Japanese—the Allies had been losing everywhere: on land, in the air, and on the sea. Just days before, the Japanese had sent an ace fighter team swooping and swirling over New Guinea.

He figured that the fighter pilots escorting the bombers back to their homeland had simply gotten cocky and careless. In any case, Morehead targeted one of the bombers and said to himself, "I'll do a slow roll for ya." He came out of the roll with his P-40 Warhawk, and ended up bagging his first Betty, riddling the plane up to the cockpit with his six 50-caliber machine guns. With no armor plating and self-sealing fuel tanks, the plane was doomed.

Then he got two more.

It was the first victory for the U.S. on any front, and because Americans were starving for good news in a thus-far depressing war,

The Curtiss P-40 Warhawk in flight. James Morehead was part of a brave band of American airmen holding the line against the Japanese onslaught early in World War II.

Morehead's feat landed him on the pages of such newspapers as *The New York Times*, the *Oakland Herald*, the *Chicago Tribune*, and the *Los Angeles Times*, among others.

In a sense, the Army and the need for pilots were a blessing, as terrible as the war itself was, for it gave Morehead the means to earn a living. Born and raised on a farm in Paoli, Oklahoma, he and his family constantly faced poverty due to drought, dust storms, and the Depression. "My father made a sad mistake; he sold a hardware store to buy a big farm." At 17, Morehead left home by catching a freight train headed west, but was kicked off by California lawmen. Turning to the highway, he was given a ride back the other way, where he ended up in Kansas.

Realizing he wasn't going anywhere with his life, Morehead returned home, where his father gave him ten acres, which he used to put in a crop of corn. Fortunately, the rains came, and he had enough money to pay for training as a flying cadet, which got him into the Army Air Corps the day after graduation on the 2nd of April, 1941.

"That luck almost compares with my luck when my unit was assigned to the Philippines. I left Hamilton Field, where I was a fighter pilot, but had a midair collision and was in the hospital. Pearl Harbor occurred, and I never quite got to the Philippines." Morehead's first encounter with the enemy was no picnic, however. "It was like Marianas Turkey Shoot… in reverse.*

"We had terrible losses."

Over a three-year span, Morehead was credited with a total of eight aerial victories by downing seven aircraft in the Pacific and one over Romania. After the war, he became a squadron commander in Italy for the 4th Air Force, and following that, was base commander of the Chico Army Air Field in California. He was then sent to Formosa (Taiwan), where he was assigned the duty of training pilots in Chiang Kai-shek's Nationalist Chinese Air Force on flying jet planes. He later served at the Pentagon until he retired as a colonel in 1967.

After his retirement from the service, Morehead and his wife Betty entered the purchase and development of real estate, including industrial parks in Petaluma, California, not far from the former airfield where he first learned to fly. Morehead was also a renowned marksman and a big game hunter with a home filled with trophies, including a cape buffalo, an African lion, a hyena, and even a grizzly bear.

James Morehead resides in Petaluma, California, his wife having passed away in September 2011.

Colonel James B. Morehead

* "The Great Marianas Turkey Shoot" was the name given by American forces to the Battle of the Philippine Sea in June 1944, in which the Japanese lost hundreds of planes and pilots.

HOLDING THE RIDGE AT GUADALCANAL

MITCHELL PAIGE Veteran

"When the trip wires went and everything broke open, there was pandemonium like you have never seen or heard. There's no way in the world I could describe the sounds."

Mitch Paige, on the relentless suicide assaults by the Japanese on Guadalcanal, from an interview with *Veterans Chronicles*

They just kept coming and coming. It was October 1942, and Allied forces—primarily the 1st Marine Division—were desperately holding onto a perimeter of land surrounding Henderson Field on Guadalcanal. The Japanese held the remainder of the 90-mile-long island and were constantly attempting to penetrate and overrun the Allied defenses.

Determined to drive the U.S. forces into the sea and retake the airfield, the Japanese battleships had bombed the American positions for days, while three infantry regiments of the enemy, some 7,000 soldiers, were busy cutting a trail through the jungle. Finally, on the 26th, the Japanese were ready and launched a fierce nighttime attack on the perimeter.

Marines rest in the field during the battle for Guadalcanal, the first major offensive by Allied forces against the Empire of Japan.

"I put a wire across my line, a few feet out in front," recalled Mitchell Paige, who was a platoon sergeant at the time. He had positioned his men on a ridge. "I placed an empty C-ration can, which I blackened and carried with me everywhere, and put an empty cartridge in it as a trip wire." When it started to rattle, he and his platoon would know that the enemy was almost on top of them.

The silence was so pervasive, the men, yards apart in their foxholes, could hear each other breathing. They waited for what was certain to come. And it did.

Mitchell Paige knew from the time he was a young boy growing up in the Camden Hills neighborhood of West Mifflin, Pennsylvania, that he wanted to be a Marine. His mother, a Serb immigrant, would remind him of his roots, but also instilled in him pride and respect for America and his country's flag. In 1936, when he was 18, he walked from his home to the nearest Marine recruiting office... which was in Baltimore, Maryland, almost 240 miles away. After bulking him up with bananas to make the weight, the Marines took him and sent him to boot camp at Paris Island, South Carolina.

Paige's first assignment as a Marine was as a machine gunner on the battleship *Wyoming* during an extended cruise through the Caribbean. On February 1, 1941, Paige was part of the 1st Marine Division, formed at Guantanamo Bay, Cuba, as Japan began to flex its muscles in the Pacific.

Guadalcanal was the first offensive test on land for the U.S. military, and on October 23, 1942, the maximum number of enemy forces and the maximum number of Marines—around 50,000 troops total—were faced off against each other. When Paige's trip wires went off, the night exploded in noise and confusion, as waves of screaming Japanese with fixed bayonets charged out of the blackness. The 33 men were facing some 3,000 Japanese. Grenades were exploding all over the top of the ridge. Dark shapes crawled along the ground.

Within minutes after the second wave burst out of the jungle, Paige was alone, the men around him either killed or wounded in their foxholes. For two hours before daybreak, he ran back and forth along the ridge from one machine gun to the next, "letting the Japanese believe before the next wave came up there were a lot of Marines up there." He added, "I guess they fell for it."

Bumping into the right flank of George Company as he raced across the ridge, Paige ordered them to fix bayonets and form a skirmish line along the ridge. Dawn was breaking and a third charge by the Japanese was imminent. Unclamping the 80-pound machine gun and grabbing two belts of ammunition, Paige charged down the slope spraying the retreating enemy in front of him with the skirmishers screaming the "rebel yell" behind him. There was nothing left to shoot at. The battle was over, and the jungle was quiet again. Hundreds of the enemy lay dead on the ridge and in the grass below.

Paige was commissioned a second lieutenant in the field on December 19, 1942, and for his incredible bravery, he was presented with the Medal of Honor by General Alexander Vandegrift in a special ceremony on May 21, 1943.

Colonel Mitchell Paige

Paige later served in the Korean War, retiring in 1959 with the rank of colonel. Afterward, he became involved in the development of miniature rockets, and took a special interest in exposing and prosecuting imposters claiming to have been awarded the Medal of Honor.

Mitchell Paige passed away on November 23, 2003, at the age of 85, leaving behind his wife Marilyn.

UNDER THE WIRE AT OMAHA BEACH

HARLEY REYNOLDS Veteran

"The fire was so intense on that beach, so many bullets flying in the air and about you, between your legs, under your arms. The bullets were like a disturbed beehive."

Harley Reynolds, on the chaos during the landings on Normandy, from an interview with *Veterans Chronicles*

Sergeant Harley Reynolds couldn't understand why he hadn't been hit. All along the beach, men were going down from machine gun fire and the shrapnel of exploding shells. He heard the hissing of bullets whizzing by him and felt the tugs at his pant legs. Somehow he made it across the hard, flat sand to the relative safety of an embankment, a raised roadway of rocks that ran parallel to the beach. Behind it, men were hunkered down, stopped by coils of barbwire that stretched across the top of the embankment.

Reynolds was determined to get through the wire, but he wasn't sure how. Most of the men carrying the cutting tools and explosives to blow the wire were already killed or wounded, and the air was filled with bullets chipping away at the rocks, as German sharpshooters took aim at the helmets of men poking their heads up for a quick look at what was in front of them.

There was nothing to do but wait with mortars and artillery shells bursting around them. Every few minutes, Reynolds would yell over the din of the battlefield, to check on the men hugging the embankment to his right. An hour went by as the pounding continued.

All of a sudden, a G.I. unknown to Reynolds crawled up beside him, lugging a Bangalore torpedo, a tube with an explosive device used for clearing a path through mines and wire. He shoved the torpedo under the barbwire, and when it failed to go off, he crawled back to wire, and replaced the igniter. He then again pulled the string, looked back at Reynolds for a brief moment, and was shot dead.

The G.I. who blew a hole in the wire so that Reynolds and his men could crawl through was never identified. "To me," Reynolds remarked, "he was the greatest hero on the beach."

For Reynolds, the beaches of Normandy were a far cry from the mountains of far western Virginia, where he grew up in the coal-mining town of St. Charles, five miles from the Kentucky state line. There he spent most of his time hunting and fishing. At 16, he was ready for something more adventurous than working in a mine or the family grocery store, and he badgered his father to sign

Though the beaches of Normandy were secured, the price of victory was high.

enlistment papers for the Army stating that he was 18. "They didn't check on you in those days."

It was another year before Pearl Harbor. When he enlisted, he was sent first to Fort Jay on Governor's Island, New York, and eventually to Camp Blanding, Florida, where his unit was told they were training to be sent to the Pacific. Then whoever makes those kinds of decisions changed their mind, and in short order, Reynolds' division was issued winter clothes and was on the *Queen Mary* headed for Scotland, where they took a train down to Tidworth Barracks to train for the invasion of Africa. From Africa, Harley Reynolds, staff sergeant of B Company, 16th Infantry, 1st Infantry Division, found himself in Gela, Sicily, and eventually on the troop ship *Samuel Chase* as part of the invasion of Normandy.

Before he hit the beach at Omaha, Reynolds "knew it was going to be bad." He explained, "The emplacements, the trenches, the preparations the Germans had made to keep us from getting on the beach" were tougher than he could have imagined. Somehow, he made it across the beach to the embankment, and thanks to the bravery of the unknown G.I., he was the first to make it through the wire, diving sideways to avoid the strands. In front of him were wire fences—one with a trip wire—a small pond, and a minefield leading up a bluff, all of which he and the men strung out behind him had to cross, enemy bullets flying around them.

Climbing carefully to avoid the mines, Reynolds made it to the top of the hill, where he could look across a draw at a large pillbox with Germans moving about in entrenchments. Setting up a machine gun, he had his gunner fire on the enemy and was joined by an outfit on the right that began to throw grenades into the trenches. Before long, white flags appeared, the Germans surrendering. As the other Americans moved in to search the trenches and pillbox and round up the prisoners, Reynolds broke down his machine gun and headed inland to catch up with the rest of his squad.

After the war, Harley Reynolds returned home, entered school under the G.I. Bill, and took up the trade of tool engineering and die design and engineering. Retired for years, he lives with his wife Dorothy in St. Petersburg, Florida.

Staff Sergeant Harley A. Reynolds

BEHIND THE LINES WITH MERRILL'S MARAUDERS

DAVID RICHARDSON Veteran

"We were hit with fatigue and jungle diseases… malaria, dysentery. You'd go to sleep next to a guy and wake up, and he'd be dead."

Dave Richardson, on capturing Myitkyina, the last major Japanese stronghold in Burma, from an interview with *Veterans Chronicles*

It had been a grueling 65-mile trek over the Kumon mountain range, 6,000 feet up under impossible conditions: soaking rains turning to steam in the stifling heat, supply mules slipping and plunging to their deaths in the valleys below, and men dropping along the way, wracked with malaria and dysentery and outright exhaustion. For Merrill's Marauders, officially known as the 5307th Composite Unit, driving the Japanese from Myitkyina and capturing the airfield would be a welcome change from the leeches and impassable trails they'd had to deal with during the past several days.

Embedded with Merrill's Marauders was an American journalist and reporter for *Yank—The Army Weekly* for enlisted men. He was there not only to write about the war in Burma, but also to fight in it, for he was a U.S. soldier, Technical Sergeant David Richardson. Why Burma? "China was alone in the Far East fighting the Japs," Richardson explained in an interview with *Veterans Chronicles*. "We needed a road pushed through that connected the old Burma Road so supplies could be brought into China by road from India."

But first, the Allies had to clear the Japanese out of Burma. The answer: a specially trained group of raiders operating behind enemy lines, destroying railroads, blowing up ammunition dumps, disrupting communications, attacking patrols, and cutting the supply lines of Japanese forces—in particular, the elite Japanese 18th Division.

Raised in Maplewood, New Jersey, Richardson's abilities as a writer and reporter became apparent in high school, when he got a job

The 5307th Composite Unit, aka "Merrill's Marauders," prior to departing Ledo, February 1944.

with a local newspaper, and later at Indiana University, where he worked his way up to editor-in-chief of the *Indiana Daily Student*.

When the war started and Richardson was drafted, he heard that *Yank* was starting up, and "I wrangled my way onto that." He was sent to the Pacific to set up the down-under edition of the magazine. *Yank* was being allowed by the military services to cover any aspect of the war in any theater.

Rather than overseeing publication of the magazine in Australia, however, Richardson chose to be a war correspondent, and once the magazine was up and running, he immediately headed for New Guinea, where the Australian troops were doing most of the fighting. Soon he was with the Army Air Force, covering bombing missions, and in what could have been an ill-fated decision, faked himself onto one of the aircraft as a waste gunner. Attacked by Japanese Zeros, the plane and he were fortunate to survive.

Next were PT boats, as Richardson had learned they were attacking Japanese shipping at night. The problem was that the convoys were accompanied by Japanese destroyers and cruisers. Wondering what chance the plywood PT boats would have against the superior guns of the enemy, he was told by Commander John Buckley, "We dash in, shoot at them [the transports] with everything we got, set them on fire, riddle them, and then get the hell out of there. We rely on speed."

Richardson may have never made it to Burma, as he was somehow able to talk his way into the first wave of the amphibious landing on Leyte. General Douglas MacArthur was making good on his promise to return to the Philippines. There, Richardson ducked into the jungle with bullets "whizzling through the trees" during the Japanese pounding of Allied troops as they hit the beach.

He lived through it, though, and after returning to the States for a while, he was on his way to Burma.

Finally emerging from the jungle, the Marauders quickly captured the lightly defended airfield. The Japanese had been caught completely by surprise. Myitkyina itself, however, was a different story, despite the help of the 150th Chinese Regiment, American intelligence having underestimated the Japanese strength there. It took a month of intense fighting before Myitkyina was finally captured. At this point, the war was winding down in Burma, and in January 1945, the road was completed, with Richardson manning a machine gun on the first tank into China.

Technical Sergeant David B. Richardson

Merrill's Marauders had walked 1,000 miles through the jungles and over the steep mountainous terrain of Burma—most of the time surviving on K-rations—and had fought in 35 engagements. Of the 2,997 men who crossed the border into Burma, only 130 combat-effective Marauders were left when they disbanded.

After the war, Dave Richardson went on to be a noted correspondent for *Time*, *Life*, and *U.S. News & World Report*. He passed away on January 25, 2005, at his home in Washington, DC.

DEADLY COMBAT OVER NORTH VIETNAM

RICHARD STEPHEN RITCHIE Veteran

"Small, silver; it left very little smoke trail. It's hard to see a MiG-21 outside of two miles, or even less sometimes. It depends on the angle, the sun... very hard to see, so that's a real problem, [and] the MiG-21 can turn tighter than an F-4."

Steve Ritchie, on the challenges of going up against the MiG-21 in a dogfight, from an interview with *Veterans Chronicles*

The mission had been called "Misty out of Phuket." Misty was the radio call sign, and Phuket was the island off the coast of Thailand where the aircraft took off and landed. Known as the Fast Forward Air Controller, or Fast FAC, program, it entailed Air Force F-100s with FAC guidance and communication systems flying over infiltration routes from Hanoi and Haiphong used by the North Vietnamese and Viet Cong to invade South Vietnam. The idea was to look for targets on the move, and if none were found during a run, bridges, oil storage facilities, and other fixed targets would do. The planes carried white phosphorous smoke rockets, used to mark the target for follow-up bombing by fighters.

It was a dangerous mission, with almost a quarter of the planes being shot down. In September 1968, a change was made... the F-100s were replaced by F-4 Phantoms with superior stability and ground attack capabilities. The first to fly an F-4 Fast FAC mission was Lieutenant Richard "Steve" Ritchie, who had been assigned to the 480th Tactical Fighter Squadron at Danang Air Base, South Vietnam. Using the call sign "Wolf," Ritchie flew 95 missions in his first tour, all in the F-4s.

Ritchie was born and raised in Reidsville, North Carolina, where he excelled in both football and academics. Despite breaking his leg twice, once in the eighth grade and again in the ninth, he went on to become a star quarterback for his high school football team. From there, he managed to get into the newly established Air Force Academy, and though he played

Then-captain R. "Steve" Ritchie pictured beside his aircraft in South Vietnam, 1972, following the mission that would make him the only Air Force "ace" pilot of the Vietnam War.

football as a starting halfback for the Falcons, of more significance to his career was a pilot indoctrination program he volunteered for, in which he spent time in a T-37, the first jet trainer. It was enough to convince him that he wanted to fly single-engine fighter planes for the Air Force.

Ritchie's football career ended with the 1963 Gator Bowl, but his military career was just beginning. Graduating from the Academy in 1964, he received his initial pilot training in the service at Laredo Air Force Base in Texas, where he finished first in his class. From Laredo AFB, he was sent to Eglin Air Force Base in Florida, and for two years, he trained on the F-104 Starfighter. He was then transitioned to the F-4C Phantom at Homestead Air Force Base in Florida in preparation for being sent overseas to Danang and his first tour of duty as a pilot flying Fast FAC missions over North Vietnam. After completing his tour of duty in the Fast FAC program, Ritchie was assigned to Air Force Fighter Weapons School at Nellis Air Force Base in Nevada as an instructor.

In 1972, Ritchie signed up for a second tour of duty, and it was during this time that he made his mark as the first Air Force ace in the Vietnam War. Assigned to the 432nd Tactical Reconnaissance Wing at Udom, Thailand, he found himself back in the pilot's seat of an F-4 (usually, an F-4D) with the 555th Tactical Fighter Squadron. In less than four months, he accomplished a feat no other Air Force pilot had done during the war—namely, to shoot down five MiG fighters, including two in one day.

To Ritchie, the F-4 was an ideal match for the MiG-21. "The advantage that the Phantom has over the MiG is that we have more power," he recalled. "So, if we're going vertical, we can zoom farther, which means the MiG has to fall off first, and we can fall off in behind it." He added, "We could also outrun it… if you really got into a bind, and we had to escape." Then, too, the F-4 also had more and better weapons… and radar, which the North Vietnamese didn't have.

Despite the advantages, the comparatively small, silver, ground-controlled interception (GCI) MiG fighters were a nimble and formidable foe in the hands of experienced pilots, for they were hard to see outside of two miles away and could maneuver with tighter turns than the F-4s.

Brigadier General R. Stephen Ritchie

In total, during his two tours of duty, Ritchie flew 339 combat missions, logging more than 800 hours of flight time. In 1974, he resigned his regular commission and held various positions in civilian life. He joined the Colorado National Guard, and in 1994, he was promoted to brigadier general in the Air Force Reserve, becoming mobilization assistant to the commander of the Air Force Recruiting Service.

Steve Ritchie retired from the service in 1999. Today, he lives in Colorado Springs, Colorado, and is a motivational speaker.

TAKING THE WAR TO THE JAPANESE HOMELAND

EDWARD SAYLOR Veteran

"We hit the water with the wheels down, and that stopped us immediately. Tore both engines out. All the other four members of the crew were thrown out through the nose. I was in the back, knocked unconscious for a short time."

Ed Saylor, on the forced landing of his B-25 bomber after running out of fuel during the Doolittle Raid, from an interview with *Veterans Chronicles*

Flight engineer Edward Saylor didn't expect to come back alive. And with good reason. There simply wasn't enough fuel to get home, which meant either ditching the B-25 or crash-landing it, most likely into the sea… and most likely in enemy-held territory. As things turned out that day, all 16 bombers were lost.

April 18, 1942. The USS *Hornet*, buffeted by rain and headwinds of 25 to 30 knots, was still 650 nautical miles out to sea from the Japanese homeland when it was sighted by a Japanese picket boat. Lieutenant Colonel Doolittle and *Hornet* skipper Captain Marc Mitscher had planned to be a lot closer before launching the 16 bombers on what has become known as the Doolittle Raid, but were concerned that the picket boat may have had time to warn Tokyo before one of their escort ships could sink it. Landing medium bombers like the B-25s on the *Hornet* was impossible, so the plan had been for the aircraft to proceed on to bases in China. Being so far out meant that was impossible.

Eighty crewmen on 16 B-25 Mitchell bombers took part in the Doolittle Raid. Three were killed with eight being taken prisoner, four of whom would die in captivity. The raid proved to be among the most celebrated moments of World War II.

And there were other problems as well. The B-25s had only a very short 464 feet of flight deck in which to make it into the air. Plus, none of the pilots had ever taken off from a carrier before. Despite the problems, however, they all got off safely and circled single-file toward Japan at wave-top level to avoid detection. None of the 80 men in the 16 bombers had any idea how—or if—they would get home. Figuring that out would need to wait until after they dropped their bombs.

Saylor was born in the rural community of Brusett, Montana, and was raised on a cattle ranch near Jordan, where he attended high school. At 19 in December 1939, he enlisted in the Army Air Corps and was sent to Fort George Wright in Spokane, Washington. He was then assigned to the Air Corps Training School at Chanute Field, Illinois, to be a mechanic.

Following training, Saylor served as a flight engineer at various bases, and in Columbia, South Carolina, where he had been assigned to the 89th Bomb Squadron, he volunteered for a top-secret mission, not knowing anything about what it was or where he was going. All he knew was that his next stop was Florida. "We were training in Eglin, trying to get the planes airborne under 500 feet," he recalled.

Following training, and still unaware of their mission, the men were sent to Alameda Naval Air Station in California, where they boarded the USS *Hornet*. It wasn't until they were at sea headed for Japan that they were told their mission.

The bombing run itself over Japan was uneventful, as the raid was a complete surprise to the Japanese military. After dropping its payload on an aircraft factory in Kobe, Japan, Saylor and the rest of the crew had to face the realization there was not enough fuel to make any of the bases in China and that ditching the plane or crash-landing it was inevitable. The pilot spotted a beach on an island off the coast of mainland China in enemy-occupied territory, but he misjudged the distance, and the plane hit the water hard, flipping over.

Unconscious for a few minutes, Saylor managed to work his way back to an escape hatch on the bottom of the plane, and climbed out safely, jumping off a wing into waist-deep water. He and the others were rescued shortly after by Chinese fishermen, who rowed them to another island and ultimately got them to the mainland, where they were turned over to the Chinese underground.

It was touch and go for several days, as the crew and their Chinese rescuers sought to stay ahead of enemy soldiers searching for them after finding the plane. A few of the crew were hurt seriously and had to be carried. Eventually, they made it into free China, where they got medical attention.

Of the 16 planes, 12 crash-landed somewhere in China, three were ditched at sea, and one crash-landed in Siberia. Eight of the 80 men were captured by the Japanese, of which three were executed and one died of

Lieutenant Colonel Edward J. Saylor

disease. Three died during the crash-landings. Sixty-nine men managed to escape capture and death.

After the raid, Saylor returned to the U.S. for a short time, working with B-26s at Eglin, before being sent overseas, where he was on 26 bombing missions over North Africa. He then spent the rest of the war in Europe working with B-26 bomber squadrons. He retired in March 1945, and returned to Montana, where he worked for the post office in Missoula.

Edward Saylor lives in Puyallup, Washington. His wife Lorraine passed away in June 2011.

LOSS OF THE USS *GAMBIA BAY*

EUGENE SEITZ Veteran

"On the day of the battle, we were in the ready room, when the skipper came on the 1MC and hollered, 'For God's sake, man your planes, the Jap fleet is on our behind.'"

Gene Seitz, on the hurried announcement by Captain Hugh Goodwin over the shipboard address system that the Japanese fleet was headed for them, from an interview with *Veterans Chronicles*

They suddenly appeared out of the early morning mist, their pagoda-like masts clearly identifying them as Japanese. Four battleships, six heavy cruisers, two light cruisers, and 11 destroyers. In front of them was the much smaller American task force known as "Taffy 3," consisting of six escort carriers, including pilot Gene Seitz's USS *Gambia Bay*, three destroyers, and four destroyer escorts.

With Admiral William "Bull" Halsey's immense 3rd Fleet off chasing the decoy carriers of the Japanese Northern Force, the still-powerful Center Force—it had taken a pounding the day before by Halsey—had slipped undetected through San Bernardino Strait past Samar Island, and was headed for Leyte Gulf, where the U.S. soldiers' invasion was underway.

The Wildcat was the only effective fighter available to the U.S. Navy and Marine Corps in the Pacific theater of World War II, helping American engineers develop aircraft to beat the Japanese Zero on its own terms.

Seitz was the first in the air in his FM-2 Wildcat. "I looked and saw more ships than I ever realized existed," Seitz recalled. "Some other planes joined me and we proceeded on up and started strafing these battleships. We usually shot for the bridge, trying to knock out glass and the commands."

The problem was that the Taffy 3 was heavily outgunned against the Japanese armada, and before long, the *Gambia Bay* was hit with an eight-inch shell that flooded her forward engine room. Critically wounded with limited power and soon dead in the water, the carrier became a direct target of the Japanese heavy cruisers, which closed to point-blank range.

Seitz knew his ship was in trouble, and he as well, when he heard through his headphones, "We are sinking. Go to Tacloban [airfield on Leyte]. Goodbye." So, now he had two problems: the Japanese fleet, and the loss of his carrier.

Seitz's interest in flying dated back to when he was in college at Fresno State. "President Roosevelt wanted 50,000 pilots. And so I was able to take a flying course as part of my college training and got a pilot's license." A second course gave him his commercial license, and he learned to fly acrobatics as well. At Oakland airport, he saw men standing in a line. When asked, they said they were going to be Naval aviation cadets. So Seitz joined the line.

From there, Seitz was sent to Pensacola, Florida, for further training, and became an instructor in instrument training. After a year and a half of teaching students to fly with instruments, he joined Squadron VC-10 and found himself assigned to the *Gambia Bay*, which proceeded to Pearl Harbor, Saipan, Tinian, and Guam, strafing enemy troop concentrations and bombing gun emplacements. From there, the *Gambia Bay* supported the landings at Guadalcanal.

After a short break in the Marshalls for logistics, the *Gambia Bay* was back at sea, supporting the amphibious attack on the islands of Peleieu and Angaur, and then to Manus Island, where General Douglas MacArthur began his return to the Philippines.

In September, the *Gambia Bay* became part of Taffy 3 and was off to Leyte Gulf. On October 25, 1944, in what became known as the Battle of Samar, the *Gambia Bay* and its small fleet of escort carriers, destroyers, and destroyer escorts were all that stood between the enemy battleships comprising the Japanese Center Force and the landing of U.S. troops on Leyte Gulf, other than the also small Taffy 2 task force stationed at the entrance to Leyte Gulf.

For Seitz, his immediate worry was the Japanese ships below him and the anti-aircraft fire coming up at him. Fortunately, the sky was soon filled with American aircraft from the *Gambia Bay* and the other escort carriers in Taffy 3, and eventually aircraft from Taffy 2 some 20 miles away. Despite the overwhelming balance of power in surface ships in favor of the Japanese Center Force, *it turned back*. Taffy 3's escort carriers, destroyers, and destroyer escorts with their torpedo attacks and the hundreds of planes circling the Japanese armada had done their job.

As Rear Admiral Thomas Sprague, commander of Taffy 3, commented in surprise, "At best, I had expected to be swimming by this time."

Captain Eugene W. Seitz

The sinking of the *Gambia Bay* marked the end of Squadron VC-10 as a unit. After the battle was over and running low on fuel, Seitz set down on Tacloban Field on Leyte. Eventually, he joined BBF-14, which was a fighter squadron, and was on his way to Japan on the fleet aircraft carrier USS *Enterprise* when the war ended. During his flying career, Seitz logged more than 6,000 hours in 55 different types of aircraft.

Eugene Seitz and his wife Jean reside in Annadale, Virginia.

RAISING THE FLAG ON IWO JIMA

DAVE SEVERANCE Veteran

"I landed with 240 men, six other officers, and seven corpsmen. I came out with 44 men. I lost all officers."

Dave Severance, on his devastating losses during the fight for Iwo Jima, from an interview with *Veterans Chronicles*

You couldn't see who was shooting at you. That was the problem—at least, one of the problems—on Iwo Jima. Captain Dave Severance and the men of Company E had no idea where the bullets and shells were coming from, for the Japanese had dug a vast network of caves and tunnels and concealed gun positions on the island, and they rarely surfaced. "They were scurrying underground," recalled Severance. "You had to figure where they were, try to get up close, and get the flamethrower and explosives in."

Defending the island were somewhat more than 21,000 diehard, tenacious Japanese, but capturing Iwo Jima and especially the airstrip on the island was essential, for American aircraft would then be within bombing range of the Japanese homeland. No other battle would prove to be more difficult, for more than half of all casualties in the Pacific suffered by the Marines occurred on Iwo Jima.

Slowly, foot-by-foot, Company E fought its way across the volcanic sand to the base of Mount Suribachi on the southern tip of the island. By then, the company had lost a third of its men, and all three of the platoon leaders had been wounded and evacuated. Looking up at the summit of the

The first flag raised atop Mount Suribachi on Iwo Jima. The flag would soon be replaced by a second, larger flag, captured in Joe Rosenthal's legendary photo.

volcano, and the steepness of the 500-foot slope to the top, Severance wasn't sure if they could climb it. He also had to have wondered what was waiting for them there and along the way up, for the mountain was clearly pockmarked with caves.

Severance was on the island to begin with because of a decision by the military to disband the 2nd Parachute Battalion he was in, since "there was no place they could drop us in the jungle."

Back in Greeley, Colorado, in the '20s and '30s, Severance was fascinated with flying, devouring pulp magazines he bought for a dime. In March or April 1941, after a year of college, a stint at sea school, and some traveling, he decided to join the paratroops.

When the Japanese attacked Pearl Harbor on December 7, 1941, Severance was a corporal, stationed at Camp Elliott, California, and within months, he was sent overseas and ultimately to New Caledonia before landing in Bougainville, where he was soon involved in firefights with the Japanese. In January 1944, he was pulled back to the States, and with the disbanding of the paratroops, he began his new career as a captain of Company E in the 28th Marine Regiment of the 5th Division.

Months later, Severance found out that he and his battalion were being trained to invade an island in the Pacific called Iwo Jima. "We didn't know where it was."

The fighting for Mount Suribachi was severe at the base and along the lower slopes, but on February 23, a four-man reconnaissance patrol from Company F made it to the top, only to find almost none of the enemy there. "When we were planning to go in there," Severance indicated in his interview with *Veterans Chronicles*, "it was our opinion if we took the mountain, the battle would end. We figured the rest of the island would fall like dominos. And of course, it turned out just the opposite."

Embroiled in a fierce and ongoing battle to clear the caves and bunkers on the mountain, Severance had little time to think about anything other than the enemy, but was ordered by the battalion commander to send a platoon up to raise an American flag on top of Mount Suribachi. As is well documented in history, hours later, the flag was replaced with a larger flag by six soldiers from Severance's company, who became as famous as the symbol of the flag itself, thanks to the photo immortalized by Associated Press photographer Joe Rosenthal. It was the most reproduced photograph of the war, even ending up on a postage stamp.

Colonel Dave E. Severance

For Severance and the three Marine divisions on Iwo Jima, the battle went on for a total of 36 days, with all but about a thousand of the 21,000 Japanese dying in defense of the island, contesting every foot of it. The losses in Company E were almost as high. Of the 271 men who landed on Iwo Jima, casualties ran from 75 percent to 80 percent. Severance, fortunately, came through unscathed, and for his bravery and leadership was awarded the Silver Star.

Dave Severance is married and lives in LaJolla, California. At age 93, he is a frequent speaker at reunions of Iwo Jima veterans and other events.

COUNTERATTACK AT BLOODY GULCH

EDWARD SHAMES Veteran

"I caught a bullet across the bridge of my nose. I jumped into a bunch of cows, and mooed like the cows did, and it saved my life."

Ed Shames, on encountering German soldiers after parachuting behind enemy lines during the early morning of June 6, 1944, from an interview with *Veterans Chronicles*

June 12, 1944. German resistance had been relatively light. The bulk of the German forces had withdrawn to the southwest, and the 101st Airborne had been able to enter Carentan without much difficulty. For Staff Sergeant Ed Shames of the 2nd Battalion of Easy Company in the 506th Parachute Infantry Regiment (PIR), however, getting there in one piece required on-the-spot creative thinking. Parachuting behind the lines at Normandy on the early morning of June 6th, he had come down far from where he was supposed to be, landing by a barn at a Carnation Milk plant outside of Carentan.

General Dwight D. Eisenhower rallies men of the 101st Airborne Division prior to their drop into Normandy in a photo taken the evening of June 5, 1944, at Greenham Common Airfield in England.

German soldiers were close by. "I caught a bullet across the bridge of my nose," Shames recalled, and he hid among the cows until the Germans moved on. Gathering a number of his men who had also landed in the area, he was able to join up with the rest of his battalion in capturing the bridges into Carentan and fighting their way into the town.

The next day, all hell broke loose. Determined to recapture Carentan to drive a wedge between the Allies moving inland from Omaha and Utah beaches, the German forces were resupplied and reinforced during the night by assault guns and mechanized infantry, and at dawn on the 13th, they attacked with a vengeance. Under the intense German fire, F Company of the 506th fell back, as did D Company on the right flank.

Holding in the middle, Easy Company was all alone.

Shames was born and raised outside of Norfolk, Virginia, "more or less in farm country." Being from Norfolk, the expectation was that he would go into the Navy, but Fort Monroe put out fliers looking for some "very, very good men" for a special unit. "I was one of the people who took the bait," Shames mentioned during the interview with *Veterans Chronicles*, and he joined the 506th. Of the 7,000 volunteers, only 2,500 would be accepted, so the Army had to weed the numbers down. "They almost killed all of us by doing it." But he made it.

Those who did were sent to a remote Army base in Taccoa, Georgia, for intense training. According to Shames, that particular location was chosen in case the "experiment" failed; no one would know about it. But it didn't fail and the 506th PIR was sent to Fort Benning, Georgia, for jump training and to Tennessee for maneuvers. Finally, they were told, "Get the hell out of here and go overseas." Soon after, they were transported to Wiltshire, England, and were attached to the 101st Airborne Division just before D-Day.

With enemy shells falling all around Easy Company outside of Carentan, Shames wondered if he was going to die on his birthday—June 13th—as the situation was looking bleak. Though D and F companies gradually moved forward on the left flank and a battalion of the 502nd took up positions on the right, the casualties were so heavy that the Germans were on the brink of breaking through the defenses.

But it didn't happen. Easy Company held long enough for the Americans to bring up 60 tanks from the 29th Division, and the counterattack forced the Germans to withdraw. Carentan and the link between the Allies moving up from Omaha and Utah beaches were secure.

That same day, Shames went from a sergeant to a second lieutenant, though he had to go back to England for a week in order for the paperwork to be processed to make the promotion official. He returned to his unit in time to make the jump into Holland, where Easy Company spent the next 77 days in an Allied operation known as Market Garden, which got bogged down when the British 1st Airborne Division ran into stronger resistance from the enemy than expected. Shames was one of the Americans selected to cross the Rhine in canvas boats to rescue what was left of the British who had made it to the other side of the river.

Colonel Edward D. Shames

From Market Garden, instead of getting the leave in Paris due him, the 101st Airborne was sent into Bastogne, Belgium, to support the 28th Infantry Division, surrounded by a superior force of German Panzers. Finally, after 29 days of snow and frigid cold, the weather broke, and C-47s dropped food, clothing, ammunition, and medical supplies on the starving soldiers inside the perimeter. Not long after, elements of General George Patton's Third Army punched through the German lines and the siege was over.

After the war, Shames stayed in the military and served in Israel, Lebanon, and Iraq, retiring with the rank of colonel.

Edward Shames and his wife Ida reside in Virginia Beach, Virginia.

TEAM JAMES AND OPERATION JEDBURGH

JOHN SINGLAUB Veteran

"We dropped at night in an area about 20 kilometers from the nearest German garrison. We jumped in uniform because of the impact it had on the French. To see an American officer was a great boost to their morale."

Jack Singlaub, on parachuting behind German lines to meet up with the French Resistance, from an interview with *Veterans Chronicles*

August 1944. Second Lieutenant John Singlaub was part of a mission known as Operation Jedburgh and was parachuting into Nazi-occupied territory in central France, where he was being met by French Resistance fighters. D-Day had begun, and Singlaub, leader of Team James, was helping to organize behind-the-lines efforts to undermine the will and ability of the German army to defeat the Allied forces.

Officially, he was under the authority of the British SOE (Special Operations Executive), but he had been recruited, screened, and trained by the U.S. Office of Strategic Services (OSS), the American intelligence equivalent of the SOE. Each Jedburgh team consisted of a commander—in this case, Singlaub—an executive officer, and a non-commissioned radio operator. Since Singlaub was an American (English-speaking), the other officer had to be French to ensure fluent communications with the Resistance, the French population, and on occasion, with the enemy. (Belgian and Dutch officers were also used in other Jedburgh operations, depending on the country being jumped into.) The radio, commonly referred to as a "Jet-Set," was essential for communicating with Special Force Headquarters in London. While the mission of the Jedburgh teams was to provide liaison and leadership to Resistance fighters, particularly welcomed by the French were the airdrops of arms and ammunition.

Singlaub's jump from a British Air Force Sterling bomber was the beginning of a distinguished and eventful career in which Singlaub

Operation Jedburgh, Team James. From left to right: Jacques le Bel de Penguilly, John Singlaub, and Anthony Denneau.

played a major role in disrupting the communications and the movement of German forces behind the lines. To maintain the secrecy of the operations, "we would join a bomber formation en route to the interior of Europe," Singlaub recalled. "At a certain point, the airplane would drop down and abort—turn around and head back, as if we had a malfunction in our engine." The plane would then fly low over its drop zone (DZ) and disgorge the Jedburgh team.

Singlaub's journey to becoming a member of the OSS wasn't planned or predetermined. Born and raised in the farming community of Independence, California, he learned to be self-reliant early on, spending "a lot of time" hunting and fishing alone in the Sierra Nevada, "with a dog perhaps."

In September 1939, as Germany was declaring war on Poland, Singlaub entered UCLA and its ROTC program. He wouldn't finish college, however, until 1958, as he ended up in the Army at Fort Benning, Georgia, where he underwent parachute and demolition training and received his commission as a second lieutenant. Unknown to him at the time was the value of the French courses he had taken in college, for while at Fort Benning, he was contacted by a major from the OSS and ended up in Washington, DC, where he was put through a series of physical and psychological tests to determine his suitability for leadership and subversive activities behind enemy lines.

Singlaub passed with flying colors, and was shipped across the Atlantic to Glasgow, Scotland, where "in a very significant moment" he was turned over by the American officer to the British and came under "complete operational control" of the SOE. From there, he was involved in multiple operations to help liberate France.

Once the Germans had been cleared out of France, Singlaub attempted to undertake a mission to rescue French citizens who had fled into the Alps, but the effort was delayed and blunted by the Russians, who at that time were looking ahead to the territory they expected to control under the occupation of Germany. Singlaub's presence in the Alps would likely impact Russia's designs on the future of Austria.

Singlaub then volunteered to go to China to help lead Chinese guerrillas against the Japanese. Just before the Japanese surrendered, he led a rescue mission by parachuting into an enemy prisoner of war camp on Hainan Island. As a result, some 400 POWs were released.

Major General John K. Singlaub

Singlaub's career was still on the rise, however, for after the war, he joined the Central Intelligence Agency (CIA), the forerunner OSS having been disbanded in October 1945. He was sent to Manchuria during the Chinese Civil War, and in 1951, he became deputy chief of the CIA station in South Korea. From there he was sent to Laos. In 1964, he became chief of the Military Assistance Command Studies and Observation Group (MACV-SOG), which oversaw paramilitary operations throughout Southeast Asia, and prior to resigning in 1978, he became chief of staff of the United Nations Command in South Korea.

Major General John Singlaub and his wife Joan reside in Franklin, Tennessee.

THROUGH THE HEDGEROWS TO SAINT-LÔ

JOHN ROBERT SLAUGHTER Veteran

"One of my men looked over and said, 'Slaughter, are we going to get through this?' I asked myself the same thing, but I couldn't let him know I was scared to death."

Bob Slaughter, on being in the first wave to land on Omaha Beach on D-Day, from an interview with *Veterans Chronicles*

He was somehow still alive. The carnage on Omaha Beach was behind him. John Robert Slaughter had been in the first wave when his company—Company D, 116th Infantry Regiment, 29th Infantry Division—fought its way through the chaos on the beach. Getting on shore had been half the problem, with bullets whizzing around him, pinging off the landing craft, and spouts of water erupting close by from the impact of artillery shells. "People were hanging onto me," recalled Slaughter, "because I'm six foot, five inches. They were underwater and grabbing hold of me in order to breathe."

American troops storm ashore under heavy German fire on Omaha Beach on the coast of Normandy, June 6, 1944.

The 116th had finally made it over the seawall and up the embankment, where they came across "a bunch of Germans behind a concrete wall firing a Nebelwerfer, a six-barrel mortar." The location of the mortar was quickly radioed in to a destroyer off-shore, and the mortar was soon knocked out.

Slaughter stood for a moment on top of the bluff while he caught his breath and took stock of the situation. His sector of the beach had been secured, but at a heavy cost. As it turned out, Company D had already lost 70 men, 20 from his hometown. Though the Germans were pulling back toward the town of Saint-Lô, they were certain to contest every inch of the way, and behind the hedgerows that lined the patchwork of fields and pathways along the way, he could expect to encounter enemy emplacements and machine guns. There was as much danger ahead as there had been behind him.

Slaughter began his military career at 16. Born in Bristol,

Tennessee, he moved with his family to Roanoke, Virginia, after his father, a lumber worker, lost his job. "We were in the Great Depression of the '30s and my family was caught up in that," he recalled. "I guess I got tired of being poor, so I joined the National Guard, and got a dollar a drill, which was the pay scale at that time for a private."

Initially sent to Camp A. P. Hill, Virginia, Slaughter spent time at Camp Blanding, Florida, and after Pearl Harbor, instead of being discharged, he found himself on the *Queen Mary*, headed for Scotland. From there, he was sent by rail down to Tidworth Barracks in southern England. "We didn't know what we were training for, but we found out a little later that we were going to spearhead the invasion of Normandy."

Then the opportunity came along to join a special Ranger group, a hit-and-run strike force, and Slaughter volunteered for the newly formed 29th Ranger Battalion. "We trained up in Achnacarry, Scotland, under the British commandos before being sent to Cornwall, England, to climb cliffs considered similar to the ones on Omaha Beach." For reasons unknown, however, his days as a Ranger were short-lived, because the battalion was suddenly disbanded in October 1943. Slaughter returned to the 116th and Company D as it was undergoing amphibious assault training.

"We had an idea we would be going into combat soon, because you could see the buildup all around us. There were thousands and thousands of soldiers getting ready for something."

In the early morning of June 6th, Company D boarded six landing craft and joined the Allied force crossing the channel for the beaches of Normandy. Operation Overlord was underway.

The fight for Saint-Lô was as tough as Slaughter expected. Delayed by lack of supplies and stiff German resistance, it took until July 3rd for elements of the 29th to advance within a couple of miles of the town, and even then, the western flank was slogging through swampy, flooded ground, while the eastern flank was under the guns of enemy-held heights, known as Hill 192. Savage fighting finally resulted in the capture of the heights, and the battle for Saint-Lô became a series of close-quarter clashes between the hedgerows, with gains per day being measured in yards. Saint-Lô finally fell on July 16th, and with it, the Allies controlled a major crossroad into the heart of Normandy.

Staff Sergeant John R. Slaughter

For its heroic action in capturing Saint-Lô, Slaughter's battalion was awarded a Presidential Unit Citation.

Severely wounded at Vire, France, Slaughter was evacuated to England, but later returned to his unit in time to participate in the Battle of the Bulge. He was honorably discharged on July 13, 1945.

After the war, he worked for a Roanoke newspaper and became chairman of a foundation that ultimately resulted in a monument to veterans of Normandy being erected in Bedford, Virginia, the town which lost more men per capita during the war than any other town or city in the country.

John Robert Slaughter passed away on May 29, 2012, in Roanoke, Virginia, and is survived by his wife Margaret.

STAYING WITH THE BOMBERS

CALVIN SPANN Veteran

"They were glad to see us. They told us we really do a good job. 'You take us all the way to the target and bring us all the way home.'"

Calvin Spann, on escorting bombers by the Tuskegee "Red Tail" fighter squadrons, from an interview with *Veterans Chronicles*

The German jet aircraft appeared suddenly in the sky ahead of him. It was March 24, 1944. Tuskegee Airman Calvin Spann had never encountered the Messerschmitts before, and he knew his group of "Red Tail" P-51 Mustangs were literally in for the fight of their lives. Spann's 100th Fighter Squadron in the 332nd Fighter Group, one of only four all-black squadrons to see combat in the Army Air Force, was escorting B-17 bombers on a mission to Berlin and back. It was only a matter of time before the Luftwaffe launched its most advanced aircraft to protect the factories and armament plants in the German capital.

Students at Tuskegee chat after a flight in their Stearman biplanes. At left is then-captain Benjamin O. Davis, Jr., squadron commander and leader of the Tuskegee Airmen.

Within seconds, the voice of acting squadron commander Roscoe Brown (profiled in this book) rang in Spann's ear, "Bogies, nine o'clock, drop your tanks and follow me."

Spann may have hesitated for only a moment or two, for the Tuskegee Airmen, noted for the red-painted tail sections of their planes, had been strictly ordered by their commander, Colonel Benjamin Davis, Jr., not to leave the bombers—ever—to chase down enemy fighters. They were to attack the enemy only when the German fighters got close enough to shoot down the Allied bombers.

But the Messerschmitt Me-262s, clearly faster than the P-51s, were a danger that couldn't be ignored. Fortunately, they had one disadvantage. "They're like a big, fast car," Spann once commented at a speaking engagement. "They take more room to turn." It was a disadvantage that Spann and Brown planned to exploit.

Fighting must have been in his blood, for Spann, who grew up in Rutherford, New Jersey, was a Golden Gloves boxing champion at age 16. He left high school a month before graduation to join the service. His father died the year Spann left school, and for a time, he helped out by working in a fast food restaurant.

Spann passed a two-year college equivalency test, but his education would need to wait. For him, there was only one choice: he wanted to be a pilot, so he volunteered for the Army Air Corps. "Most of my friends," he once said, "were drafted. In order for me to get to where I wanted to go, I would have to volunteer."

Sent first to Kessler Field in Mississippi, he was told when arriving there that the Army did not train black cadets. So, it was on to the Tuskegee Airfield in Tuskegee, Alabama, where he learned to fly P-40 fighters. The training facility there was actually an experiment in training blacks as pilots and navigators, an experiment that was remarkably successful, as the Tuskegee Airmen compiled a remarkable record of 261 enemy aircraft shot down and 148 aircraft damaged. The 332nd alone earned as many as 1,000 awards and decorations in a little over a year of combat.

After basic training, Spann was sent to Walterboro, South Carolina, for overseas training. He was in a P-47 Thunderbolt out over the ocean, shooting at targets pulled by a target plane. Roscoe Brown became one of his mentors, telling him, "Look kid, you just fly my wing, and we'll be all right." Six months later, Spann was on his way to Naples, Italy, and then was trucked across the country to Ramitelli Airfield on the Adriatic coast, where Spann's 100th Fighter Squadron, as well as the other two squadrons of the 332nd Fighter Group, was stationed.

As the bombers neared Berlin, and as the Messerschmitt began to circle toward its target, with Brown taking the lead, the smaller, more maneuverable Mustangs cut inside the circle and looped around, coming up on the enemy in front of them. Blasting away with their machine guns, the Me-262 was soon in flames with the pilot ejecting himself from the cockpit. As Brown was known to have riddled the aircraft, he was given credit for the "kill."

At the war's end, Spann had flown 26 missions, 20 high-altitude flights protecting bombers, and six reconnaissance missions, often flying at treetop levels to avoid radar. After the war, Spann returned home and attempted to get a job as a commercial pilot… to no avail. "That was one of the most disappointing things in my career," he has remarked. "I thought I was one of the best pilots, but I couldn't get a job because of the color of my skin."

Lieutenant Calvin J. Spann

Spann ended up working for Universal Oil for 20 years and followed that with a 20-year career in pharmaceutical sales. He is a frequent quest speaker at various events around the country.

Calvin Spann and his wife Gwenelle reside in Allen, Texas.

MASTERING THE ART OF INTERROGATION

GUY STERN Veteran

"All the skills we had learned, we applied right on the first day of coming off the LSD [Loading Ship, Dock]. A soldier who saw us coming in shouted, 'Get over here Stern. We've got far too many prisoners.'"

Guy Stern, on interrogating German prisoners at Omaha Beach, from an interview with *Veterans Chronicles*

On June 9, 1944, Guy Stern found himself on Omaha Beach. Only days earlier, thousands of Allied soldiers were fighting their way off the beach and up the embankments under intense machine gun fire and the hail of artillery raining down them. This morning, with the invasion moving inland, Stern set up shop on the beach out of crates—a place to sit and an interrogation table. As soon as he did, "there was my first prisoner," he recalled.

Assigned to Team 41 of the 1st Army Headquarters, his immediate concern was obtaining tactical information: What's ahead? Where are the gun emplacements? What do the Germans have for tanks? Where are the Panzers?

Guy Stern (left) with fellow "Ritchie Boys," Jewish immigrants who were trained in intelligence and interrogation.

Stern's background and skills were essential to the invasion, for he was a German-born Jew, who had immigrated to America during the rise of the Hitler's Third Reich. Drafted in 1942, he became a sergeant in a special intelligence unit known as the "Ritchie Boys," a unit trained in interrogation techniques at Camp Ritchie, Maryland. Raised in a German household, Stern spoke the language fluently. Training taught him what to ask, and how.

Disembarking the LSD (Loading Ship, Dock), Stern had a double reason to be scared. Like any other soldier, he wanted to do his job well, and survive. Plus, as a Jew—especially one who had left his homeland—he knew things would not go well for him, if he were captured.

Stern was born in Hildesheim, Germany. The oldest child and the only son, he was sent by his worried parents in 1937 to America, where he was taken in by his uncle in St. Louis, Missouri, who had emigrated earlier from Germany. He went to high school in St. Louis and afterward studied for two years at the University of St. Louis before entering the Army in 1942.

Stern's dream from the time he reached America was to join the fight against Hitler and the Nazis and to rescue his parents. In his mind, the invasion gave him that opportunity. As Stern moved through France and into Germany behind the advancing Allies, he became more skilled as an interrogator, which gained him important information.

One of the techniques he developed with an assistant was a form of "good guy/bad guy" questioning. This particular method was intended to instill fear into the German prisoners. According to Stern, "The biggest fear of all was being turned over to the Russians." Having scrounged up a Russian uniform, Stern got a liaison officer who spoke Russian, German, and English to create a sign that he put up on the outside of his tent. He then cut out a picture of Stalin, had it framed, and then displayed it in the tent.

The assistant played the good guy. When the prisoner would say he couldn't talk about something, he was told, "I am so sorry you won't cooperate, because we just got orders from headquarters that any prisoner who doesn't cooperate is to be turned over to the Russian liaison officer, who will send you to the Soviet Union." Then the assistant would take the prisoner over to Stern, who would shout a few obscenities in German with a heavy Russian accent. The German prisoner almost always choose in the end to cooperate, especially after he was allowed to send a "last letter home" through the Red Cross.

One of the major breakthroughs for Stern was the interrogation of Dr. Wilhelm Schuebbe, captured in May 1945. Schuebbe turned out to be a Nazi doctor who admitted to Stern that he had more than 20,000 people killed because he felt they were unfit to live.

Ultimately, Stern made it back to his hometown of Hildesheim, but it was in ruins and his house was gone. He later found out that his family had been sent to the Warsaw Ghetto, and he never saw them again.

After the war, he returned to the U.S. to continue his studies. He became an instructor in German language and literature at Columbia University and later taught at the universities of Cincinnati and Maryland. He has written and edited several books on German literary history, and for 25 years until his retirement in 2003, served as distinguished professor of German literature and history at Wayne State University.

Guy Stern resides with his wife Susanna in West Bloomfield, Michigan.

Master Sergeant Guy L. Stern

© A. Lee Bennett, Jr

DITCHING OF THE "RUPTURED DUCK"

DAVID THATCHER Veteran

"We hit the water with the wheels down, and it immediately turned us over. All the other four members of the crew were thrown out through the nose. I was in the back of the plane—knocked unconscious for a short while."

David Thatcher, on the ditching of the "Ruptured Duck" after bombing Tokyo during the Doolittle Raid, from an interview with *Veterans Chronicles*

The B-25 was flying so low on its approach to Tokyo that it wasn't noticed by the six enemy fighters passing overhead. It was April 18, 1942. Soon, the navigator had the target lined up, the plane releasing its load of bombs on the Nippon Steel Factory below, as the "Ruptured Duck" arced away from Japan's capital city and headed out to sea. "We did not fly over land, but we kept within sight of land," recalled engineer and gunner David Thatcher, as the plane attempted to reach a safe landing spot in China.

It would not make it. None of the 16 planes would. All would end up either ditching in the ocean or crash-landing in a remote location. The men aboard the planes in the Doolittle Raid had known ahead of time that they would be out of fuel before they could reach a landing field.

Originally, the plan was to fly off the aircraft carrier, the USS *Hornet*, from within 450 to 500 miles of the mainland of Japan, which would give them a fighting chance at landing safely in China. But the carrier had been spotted by Japanese fishing boats a couple of hundred miles farther out from the mainland, and Admiral William Halsey couldn't take a chance that fighter planes from the task force had been successful at sinking the boats before they alerted the Japanese military. Rather than abort the mission, however, he ordered the planes to take off immediately.

Before long, all 16 planes—including Crew No. 7 of the "Ruptured Duck"—had successfully made it off the short runway of the *Hornet* into a stiff wind and were in the air headed for Japan.

One of the 16 B-25 Mitchell bombers takes off from the USS *Hornet* en route to the Japanese home islands during the Doolittle Raid.

After dropping the bombs, the mission for the B-25s became one of survival, and with the fuel on the "Ruptured Duck" critically low, pilot Ted Lawson scanned below him and saw what might be a possible spot to set down, a strip of beach along an island. Though they would still be in Japanese-held territory, they might escape detection long enough to reach friendly villagers in China. Unfortunately, in the dark and rain, Lawson missed the beach, and the plane flipped over, ejecting crewmembers, stripping the engines from the wings, and crushing the top part of the B-25. Thatcher was caught inside with water flooding in through the shattered turret.

Thatcher was raised in Bridger, Montana. After high school, he enlisted in the Army in December 1940 and attended Lincoln Airplane Mechanics School at Lincoln, Nebraska, and then went on to serve as a mechanic with the 95th Bomb Squadron in the 17th Bomber Group.

When the opportunity came up—though he had no idea what the top-secret mission was all about—Thatcher volunteered for the Doolittle Raid. He may have had some second thoughts about his choice as he regained consciousness inside the flooding, flipped-over B-25.

Fortunately, Thatcher was able to push the escape hatch open on the bottom of the plane and crawl along the outside of the belly of the plane until he could step off into waist-high water. Of the crewmembers, only he had no serious injuries, so he took over efforts to move inland to some degree of safety, for he knew a Japanese patrol boat would soon discover the plane and before long, the enemy would be searching through the jungle.

Making a pallet of bamboo tied with rope for the most serious of the injured, including the pilot, who had a deep gash on his leg, Thatcher got the men moved to a nearby village on the island. Thatcher had done his best to close the wound on the leg with used handkerchiefs, as well as "dirty old rags" provided by the Chinese to bandage other wounds. The next day, Thatcher managed to get the crew across the island and over to the mainland of China using sampans provided by the villagers. A day later, they reached a hospital.

While unfortunately Lawson's leg had to be amputated at the hospital, Thatcher's quick action in caring for the men and moving them inland and over to the China mainland avoided their capture, for they later learned that the Japanese had a patrol of some 65 soldiers scouring the island for the crew. In time, all of Crew No. 7 made it back to the U.S.

Staff Sergeant David J. Thatcher

After the Doolittle Raid, Thatcher later served in England and Africa, where he was a gunner on a B-26, before ending the war on a stateside assignment in California. Discharged in July 1945, he studied forestry at the University of Montana, and eventually went to work for the U.S. Postal Service.

David Thatcher and his wife Dawn reside in Missoula, Montana.

BLACK HAWK DOWN IN MOGADISHU

KENNETH THOMAS Veteran

"When we got to the crash site, it took quite a bit of time to get the [pilot] out. We kind of holed up. We had been in different pockets of fighting, up and down the street, and down a two-block radius, all the night."

Keni Thomas, who as an Army Ranger attempted to rescue the men who crashed in a Black Hawk helicopter on the streets of Mogadishu, from an interview with *Veterans Chronicles*

October 3, 1993. The dirt being kicked up by the Black Hawk helicopter was causing a brown-out, and squad leader Staff Sergeant Keni Thomas had to hang out of the side to see where they were landing. As soon as the bird touched down, Thomas and the men of Company B were off and running, for the Task Force Rangers were taking fire from the streets both in front of them and behind them.

The overall objective of sending Rangers into Somalia had been to stop the flow of mortar rounds and other weapons to the elusive warlord Mohammed Farrah Aidid, who had also been attacking American troops guarding United Nations food shipments. While they were looking to capture him, if possible, Company B was charged with the responsibility of dropping down into the center of Mogadishu in what is called the Barkara Market and seizing some "bad guys"—leaders of the Habr Gidr clan—holed up in a building across from the Olympic Hotel. The plan was for the helicopters to go in first. A reaction force waiting elsewhere in the city would then drive up with trucks, the prisoners would be loaded into them and carted off, and the Rangers would exfiltrate the city.

Keni Thomas and fellow U.S. Army Rangers who took part in Operation Gothic Serpent, the Battle of Mogadishu, whose story was later told in Black Hawk Down.

At first, the mission went well. "We had gotten the 12 bad guys who were in the building," Thomas recalled, and they were sent off, all in about a half hour. But suddenly, the mission changed.

Two Black Hawk helicopters were shot down by RPGs (rocket-propelled grenades), one five or six blocks away. To get to it, secure the crash site, rescue those still alive, and remove any bodies would mean fighting their way from building to building and street to street, against an enemy that included armed women and children.

In reaching the downed helicopter, the Rangers and a combined Special Operations task force sent in to help came under increasingly heavy fire from around the corners of buildings, from alleys, out of windows, and over fences… and casualties began to mount. Of the 150 U.S. troops sent into Mogadishu, over 70 percent would be wounded or killed before they could be extracted.

For Thomas, it was a rough introduction to combat, but he was destined to be a Ranger, for his father was one before him. As he has said, "I volunteered as a Ranger, fully knowing the hazards of my chosen profession." Thomas was raised in Gainesville, Florida, attended high school there, and graduated from the University of Florida. He enlisted in the Army in 1991 and went through basic training at Fort Benning, Georgia, followed by Advanced Individual Training (AIT), Airborne School, and then the Ranger School. He later went through a number of other programs (Belgian Commando School, Special Forces Combat Diver's School, the Army's Jumpmaster Course, etc.). He was assigned to serve in Company B of the 3rd Battalion in the 75th Ranger Regiment.

Bogged down by the gunfire in the area of the downed helicopter, hours went by as the men struggled to secure cover, Thomas and another Ranger lying down behind a dead mule at one point. Overhead, helicopters were dropping supplies and ammunition and spotting the positions of the enemy.

As day turned into night, the dead and wounded were collected in a building and placed in a back room, Thomas fully expecting RPGs to come ripping through the front of the building. Since no one had thought the daytime mission would take longer than an hour or two, the task force was without night vision equipment. Looking into the dark, all Thomas could see was moving shadows, and he knew that if they fired, the enemy could pinpoint their positions.

Finally, some 18 hours after the mission began, help arrived. A reaction force consisting of the rest of the Rangers plus "cooks, medics, everybody that could put a flak jacket on," along with Pakistani and Malaysian troops and the U.S. 10th Mountain Division, managed to convoy its way through to the beleaguered task force. "Then we loaded up all our casualties and sent them off. And the rest of us footed it out."

Staff Sergeant Kenneth M. Thomas

The mission, later called the Battle of Mogadishu, became the subject of the 2001 film *Black Hawk Down*. Keni Thomas is known today as a popular and successful country and western singer, along with his band Cornbread, his interest in music stretching all the way back to his choir teacher in church when Thomas was a young boy.

Kenneth Thomas resides in Dixon Springs, Tennessee.

AMBUSH AT CHAKAK, AFGHANISTAN

WILLIAM TOMLIN Veteran

"There was an alleyway that was about 100 meters long that we couldn't cover with our machine guns, and they were able to move up that alleyway and get to about 15 meters from a couple of our trucks."

Bill Tomlin, on his platoon of 45 men being ambushed by about 300 Taliban fighters in the village of Chakak, from an interview with *Veterans Chronicles*

April 9, 2007. The ten Army Humvees approached the village of Chakak, Afghanistan, in Helmand Province. The 1st Battalion, 508th Infantry Regiment of the 82nd Airborne Division was on a reconnaissance mission, and leading the 45-man platoon was Sergeant First Class William Tomlin. The scout platoon had already been in firefights for three days, the battalion having been engaged in attempting to clear the Taliban out of the province.

At mid-morning, the temperatures were already approaching 120 degrees as the caravan arrived at the top of the hill overlooking the village. Stopping there, the platoon was ordered by Tomlin to establish a secure perimeter. "We started going around to the houses that were closest to us, clearing them," he recalled. "We noticed there wasn't anybody in any of them, and that's pretty common, if you're about to be engaged."

He then set up a sniper team to look for signs of the Taliban, and shortly after, the men came under heavy fire from machine guns and RPGs (rocket-propelled grenades), as the enemy moved closer and attempted to maneuver around the platoon, even closing within 15 meters (about 50 feet) up an alleyway directly in front of Tomlin's position. The platoon had been ambushed by a large force of Taliban, and it was clear that the Taliban were getting too close. Unless they were pushed back down the alleyway, the platoon could be overrun.

Raised in Barkhamsted, Connecticut, Tomlin was a good student and an excellent athlete at Northwestern Regional No. 7 High School, where he played baseball and was on the wrestling team. His father

The war in Afghanistan has been marked by operations in often remote areas against a tenacious foe familiar with the terrain.

installed fire prevention systems for a living, while his mother worked for a defense company. At Central Connecticut State University, Tomlin worked toward a degree in actuarial science, but found paying for college difficult. To help financially, he joined the National Guard.

After college, "I didn't really feel like I was ready to join corporate America yet, so I decided to join the Army and told myself that it would just be for three years... just to go and have a little bit of fun and a little bit of adventure," Tomlin said in his interview with *Veterans Chronicles.* "Turns out," he added, "that I really liked it, so I decided to stick around for a while."

Tomlin's first deployment, once he went on active duty, was in January 2003, when he was first sent to Afghanistan. After two subsequent deployments to Iraq, he was back in Afghanistan in January 2007. Three months later, he and his platoon were facing what would turn out to be some 300 "bad guys," six times the number of men in his platoon. What's more, included in the platoon were intelligence people, Air Force joint tactical air controllers, and a mortar unit. "As far as the infantrymen on the ground, I only had about 28."

Tomlin had two immediate problems. First, he had to clear the alleyway, and quickly, before the enemy had a chance to mount a surge and overwhelm the platoon. As he observed, "At 15 meters, it's anybody's game... we don't have the advantage." The ability to shoot better was being lost as the enemy got closer. At the same time, he had to prevent the Taliban from outflanking the platoon.

Addressing the first problem required aggressively counterattacking down the alleyway with grenades and small arms fire, as the platoon gradually pushed the Taliban back down the hill and into the village. As for the problem of being outflanked, Tomlin called for reinforcements, with platoons being positioned on hills to the north and south of the village. Effective fire from both quarters and from the air took its toll on the enemy, which retreated into the poppy fields and houses in the village.

But then, after six hours of fighting in the exhausting heat, the platoon began to run low on ammunition. Informed that it would be another 24 hours before the platoon could be resupplied, Tomlin made the decision to break off the attack. The platoon had managed to defeat a force of some 300 Taliban with only 45 men, eliminating 50 of the enemy—including two Taliban leaders—*without losing a man.*

Master Sergeant William C. Tomlin III

After the engagement, Tomlin remained in Afghanistan for almost another year. All totaled, he was deployed seven times, four times to Afghanistan and three times to Iraq. Promoted to master sergeant, today he is an operational advisor for the Asymmetric Warfare Group at Fort Meade, Maryland.

William Tomlin III currently resides with his wife Sarah in Glen Burnie, Maryland.

TRAFFIC COP ON OMAHA BEACH

JOSEPH VAGHI Veteran

"It was my responsibility to control the movement of men and materials from the water up to the high water mark on the beach. You did what your training told you to do, and what your instincts told you to do."

Joe Vaghi, on landing at Omaha Beach on D-Day, from an interview with *Veterans Chronicles*

The explosion of the German artillery shell knocked him unconscious. Charging down the ramp of Landing Craft 88, Beachmaster Joseph Vaghi of the 6th Naval Beach Battalion had quickly waded ashore and taken off running across the hard-packed sand exposed by the low tide. Around him, rifle fire and machine gun bursts were pinging off the stanchions sunk along the shore to slow the advance, while German mortars were blowing geysers of water into the air and blasting holes in the beach.

It was 7:30 in the morning, and the invasion of Omaha Beach had begun.

When Vaghi came to, he discovered that his clothes were on fire and he was wounded in the knee. Putting the flames out and pulling himself together, he began to organize the movement of thousands of men and tons of materiel pouring onto the beach. He first directed his attention to removing cans of gasoline from a burning Jeep before they exploded.

Then-ensign Joseph Vaghi chats with residents of Colleville-Sur-Mer in June 1944 after Allied forces stormed the Normandy beaches during D-Day.

As beachmaster, Vaghi had two jobs. First, for his sector of the beach, getting the men, as well as vehicles and supplies, safely ashore and *off* the beach was essential. And as crucial was that of evacuating the wounded as quickly as possible. Both seemed insurmountable, for the attack was bogging down, prevented from moving forward by barbwire and minefields. And under the devastating fire of the enemy, the wounded were piling up on the beach. All around him, men were dying.

Vaghi was born and raised in the small town of Bethel, Connecticut. He was one of the five out of six brothers who were all in the service at the same time, and when the sixth one was finally old enough, he also joined up at the end of the war. From high school in Danbury, Connecticut, Vaghi earned a football scholarship to Providence College. He then went to midshipmen's school at the University of Notre Dame, where he was commissioned as an ensign in the Navy in April 1943.

At the time, the Allies were finishing up defeating the Germans in North Africa and moving on to Italy. There was talk of opening a second front in Europe with a massive assault on Hitler's forces in France. Given his choice, Vaghi would have preferred to be assigned to a destroyer, but most of the midshipmen in his class were being asked to train for amphibious operations, so he figured something was up. He was assigned first to the Philadelphia Navy Yard, and was then transferred to a beach battalion group in Norfolk, Virginia, which trained extensively, making landings at various locations along the Virginia coast.

After four or five months, he was sent to Fort Pierce, Florida, where he trained with counterparts in the Army. "We lived the Army life and dressed like Army people," Vaghi indicated in an interview with *Veterans Chronicles*. "For all intents and purposes, we were an Army organization. We learned how to use rifles, pistols, Tommy guns, all the activities the landing party would need to be proficient in."

In January 1944, he was on a transport to England. The destination was Slapton Sands, a location considered to most closely resemble the beaches of Normandy. There, 2 million men and 16 million tons of supplies slowly came together before being disbursed into "marshalling areas" along the coast. "Once there," Vaghi recalled, "you couldn't get out. Only people with the highest security clearance could." As beachmasters, "we would go to tents to discuss the operation. We knew where we were going, but not when."

The "when" was June 6, 1944. As Vaghi looked around at the chaos on the beach, he was calm and focused, for he had been well trained and he knew what to do. Using flags and blinkers, Vaghi and his team "were the only communication between the shore and the ship, and we were sending messages like crazy." Holes were finally blown in the barbwire with Bangalore torpedoes, and the men poured through, hustling their way up the embankments. Gradually, order came to the beach as the war moved inland.

Lieutenant Commander Joseph P. Vaghi, Jr.

Above the high water mark, the responsibility was no longer Vaghi's, for the Army took over. Despite being wounded and the continuous pounding from German artillery, he had remained on the beach doing his job, in his words, as a "traffic cop." After 23 days in Normandy, Vaghi returned to the U.S., but was back in action in the spring of 1945 during the landing at Okinawa in the Pacific.

After the war, Joseph Vaghi attended the Catholic University School of Architecture and became an architect. He passed away on August 25, 2012, in Kensington, Maryland.

HIROSHIMA ON A "SILVER PLATE"

THEODORE VAN KIRK Veteran

"I want you as group navigator. I can't tell you what we are going to do, but I can tell you if it works, we are going to either win or shorten the war."

Dutch Van Kirk, on being asked by pilot Paul Tibbets to join the crew of the *Enola Gay* during its dropping of the atomic bomb on Hiroshima, from an interview with *Veterans Chronicles*

August 6, 1945. It was 2:45 a.m. Tinian time when the *Enola Gay*, piloted by Colonel Paul Tibbets and navigated by Captain Theodore Van Kirk, lifted off the runway into the early morning sky over the Mariana Islands. The B-29 had been stripped of everything non-essential to the mission. Gone were the turrets, and except for the tail guns, the plane posed little threat to enemy aircraft. Fortunately, it was late in the war, and the Japanese had few fighters to challenge Allied aircraft.

In place of the 6,000 pounds of weight that had been removed was a bomb weighing 9,000 pounds, dubbed "Little Boy." This would be the first use of an atomic bomb in combat, and no one knew for sure what would happen to the plane that dropped it. Some said the shockwaves of the bomb, when it exploded, could reach eight or nine miles in the air, and there were those involved with the project who even predicted that the *Enola Gay* would be destroyed.

The mission: drop the bomb on Hiroshima, a city of 250,000 people on the Japanese homeland. Unfortunately for the people living and working there, it encompassed 100 identified military targets, including the army's military headquarters charged with the defense of Japan in the event of an invasion.

Onboard the *Enola Gay*, there was relative calm among the 12 crewmembers. Some were reading and others were taking naps. Final

The *Enola Gay* comes to a full stop upon its return from its fateful mission to Hiroshima.

assembly of bomb had been delayed until the plane was in flight, as it had been considered too dangerous to load an active atomic bomb on the plane in case the aircraft should crash upon take-off. Six and a half hours later, Hiroshima appeared some 30,700 feet below them. Van Kirk, known as "Dutch" to his friends, had brought them to within 15 seconds of the planned drop time. Bombardier Tom Ferebee peered through his Norton bombsight and at 9:15 a.m. Tinian time, "Little Boy" was unloaded over the city.

Forty-three seconds later, the shockwave reached the *Enola Gay*.

Van Kirk was born in Northumberland, Pennsylvania. As a teenager, he rowed flats of coal down the Susquehanna River for his father and worked in a grocery store. After high school, he attended Susquehanna University before joining the Army Air Force Aviation Cadet Program in October 1941. Graduating from navigation school, Van Kirk was commissioned a second lieutenant at Kelly Field, Texas. He was then assigned to the 96th Bomb Group, the first operational B-17 unit in England. The crew of his aircraft, known as the *Red Gremlin*, included both Tibbets and Ferebee, the men he would work most closely with during the flight of the *Enola Gay*. They flew 11 missions together out of England, and in November 1942, they ferried General Dwight D. Eisenhower to Gibraltar to command the North African invasion forces.

After returning to the United States, Van Kirk served as an instructor navigator before being handpicked by Tibbets to be the group navigator of the 509th Composite Group. From November 1944 to June 1945, they trained continually for the top-secret atomic bomb drop on Japan.

To pull this off, Tibbets could have pretty much what he wanted. "We had a code name—'Silver Plate'—in the 509th Group," recalled Van Kirk. "If it was a man he wanted, he could ask under the code name. If he wanted airplanes, he'd get them by invoking 'Silver Plate.' Anything of that type. Silver Plate was the highest priority."

The question was, were they going to survive the blast? After dropping the bomb, Tibbets immediately banked hard to the right in a sharp 155-degree turn and flew away from Hiroshima as fast as he could. The plane didn't get too far before a bright flash—the intensity of ten suns—could be seen extending high in the sky through their goggles, and the tail gunner reported excitedly what appeared to be a huge heat wave racing toward them. Within seconds, the *Enola Gay* was rocked by the shockwave, the plane's sheet metal rattling like it was being shaken. The city had completely disappeared under a cloud of smoke and fire and debris.

Major Theodore J. Van Kirk

Thirteen hours after it had taken off, the *Enola Gay* touched down back on Tinian. Three days later, a second bomb was dropped, this time on Nagasaki, and the Japanese surrendered. The war was over.

Van Kirk returned home after the war in August 1946. He went on to receive his bachelor and master of science degrees in chemical engineering from Bucknell University, and went to work for a major chemical company, retiring from there after 35 years.

Dutch Van Kirk and his wife Imogene reside in Stone Mountain, Georgia.

CAPTURE AND ESCAPE FROM CORREGIDOR

EDGAR WHITCOMB Veteran

"We were there 18 days before deciding to escape. We decided our chances to survive weren't good. We went out with a work detail and hid in a foxhole when the guard was looking the other way."

Ed Whitcomb, on his attempt with Marine Lieutenant Bill Harris to escape from capture on Corregidor, from an interview with *Veterans Chronicles*

Shrapnel covered the ground like snow. For 27 days, the Japanese had bombed and strafed Corregidor relentlessly. Second Lieutenant Edgar Whitcomb had escaped from Bataan just as the island was surrendering, and had crossed over to Corregidor in a boat, thinking he might find a way to continue on to Australia. It was only a matter of time before the Japanese landed troops on the island, and Corregidor, he knew, could not possibly hold out much longer. Most of the island was in shambles; the buildings had all been demolished, and the beach defenses had been bombarded to the point where the Americans were reduced to machine guns and a few mortars not yet knocked out.

Then, on the night of May 5, 1942, as Whitcomb had expected, the Japanese came ashore in waves, and before long, firefights raged along the beaches and inland as the enemy began to overwhelm the American defenses. It was over in a day, and among the prisoners was Whitcomb. The Japanese lined up the Americans, taking everything they had on them… wallets, money, etc. "They didn't know what to do with us," Whitcomb once recalled in an interview. So after marching them back and forth around the island, the Japanese ended up enclosing them in a field about the size of three or four city blocks. About 11,000 American and Filipino prisoners were crowded into the enclosure.

Whitcomb was born and raised in Hayden, Indiana, and after high school, he entered Indiana University in 1939 to study law. As the U.S. edged closer to war, he left school to join the Army as a navigator.

The infamous Bataan Death March, which resulted in the deaths of hundreds of American and thousands of Filipino prisoners of war. Through his daring escape, Edgar Whitcomb was able to avoid the fate of many of his comrades.

Deployed to the Pacific, he was at Clark Field in the Philippines on December 7, 1941, when 54 Japanese bombers flew over Oahu, destroying American warships at Pearl Harbor and the B-17s on the ground. Accompanying the bombers were 50 Zeros which strafed the flight line and shot at anything that moved.

The next day, Clark Field was under attack from a wave of enemy bombers, and Whitcomb was forced to dive into a trench as explosions rocked the ground around him. Again, the Zeros followed up by repeatedly strafing the field at treetop level and destroying anything that might get off the ground. A second wave of fighters finished the job and left the base in ruins.

Pearl Harbor, Bataan, and now Corregidor. Whitcomb was determined to escape, and after 18 days managed to convince Marine Lieutenant Bill Harris to go with him.

"We went out with a work detail and hid in a foxhole when the guard was looking the other way," Whitcomb recalled. They stayed there until dark and then began to swim through shark-infested waters toward Bataan by following what they saw for lights. When a storm came up, they got separated for a time, but somehow managed to find each other. The problem was that the lights they ended up following took them back to Corregidor.

After resting, a second nighttime swim brought Whitcomb to the mainland of Luzon, where he walked into the hills for three days, looking for food and drinking from mountain streams. Eventually, he was betrayed by Filipinos on the island, who put him in a Spanish dungeon in Manila. Fortunately, before he was captured, he had stripped off his military insignias and had adopted the name of a mining official named Robert Fred Johnson.

Nevertheless, over the period of 18 days, he was interrogated and beaten daily, at least once with an iron pipe. "At first, it was devastating," he once said. But after being hit a few times, "I was numb."

Eventually, his captors must have come to accept that he was actually a mining engineer, for Whitcomb never contradicted himself and was able to build a credible story of his life as Johnson. In any case, after the 18 days, he was put in a staff car and taken to the University of St. Thomas, which was being used as a civilian internment camp. After about a year, he was sent to Hong Kong and exchanged.

Colonel Edgar D. Whitcomb

Returning to the U.S., he was met by the FBI and put on a train to Washington, DC, where he was interviewed by intelligence and then by the Pentagon. Eventually, he was reassigned to the Philippines in a B-25 crew and left active service in 1946.

After the war, Whitcomb got his law degree and was elected to the Indiana State Senate. He resigned after three years to begin his own law practice. In 1966, he was elected secretary of state, and in 1969, the 43rd governor of Indiana.

Edgar Whitcomb resides in a rustic cabin on the Ohio River near Rome, Indiana.

BREAKOUT AT CHANGJIN

WARREN WIEDHAHN Veteran

"All at once, the ridge erupted. We heard bugles and whistles. Then we saw them—literally thousands of Chinese in their camouflage white uniforms streaming down the side of the hill. And as they came with their guns, they were shooting."

Warren Wiedhahn, on the surprise attack by the Chinese at Chosin Reservoir in a brutal 17-day battle, from an interview with *Veterans Chronicles*

November 27, 1950. The dawn was breaking in a crystal-clear sky. But it was cold. At -32 degrees, everything was frozen solid, not just the trails and the lake. It was so cold that the lubrication in the guns of the 1st Marine Division gelled, and the firing pins would jam from time to time. Batteries for the vehicles went dead quickly, movement stalled, and communications became difficult with radios that failed to operate.

Chosin Reservoir (real name "Changjin") in North Korea was not a pleasant place to be, and after spending a frigid night at a two-person outpost on top of a ridge looking off at the sprawling man-made reservoir in the distance, Sergeant Warren Wiedhahn of the 5th Marine Regiment of the X Corps and fellow soldier Charlie Riggs were more than ready to return to the rear, where they could try to get warm.

General MacArthur's daring landing at Inchon in September 1950 turned the tide in the United Nations' favor in the early days of the Korean War.

Suddenly, the sound of bugles and whistles filled the air. Looking out over the valley below, the ridge on the opposite side exploded with men in white streaming down the ridge and charging toward them, guns firing. Tens of thousands of Chinese had managed to cross the Yellow River and enter North Korea undetected by the United Nations forces. (As Wiedhahn later found out, they had traveled light and at night. They transported what they needed for ammunition and supplies in hand-drawn carts, and wiped out their tracks with pine boughs. They hunkered down in wooded groves during the day.)

Opposing what turned out to be almost 70,000 men in the Chinese 9th Corps was less than half that number—mostly the X Corps with some elements of the ROK (Republic of Korea) I Corps—and it wasn't long before the Americans and the ROK were completely surrounded.

As Wiedhahn indicated in his interview with *Veterans Chronicles*, the immediate problem was for them to "get out of there." They shot off what they had for mortar ammunition and quickly fell back. As he recalled, "It was a human wave attack."

Born in Lock Haven, Pennsylvania, and an ardent skier, Wiedhahn was used to cold winters, but certainly not the wind-blown ridges and deep penetrating cold of the mountains in North Korea. After graduating from high school in Canajoharie, New York, he enlisted in the Marines and went to boot camp at Paris Island, South Carolina. He was then sent to Quindao, China, where he served until the country fell to the Communists in 1949, and then returned on a troop ship to Camp Pendleton, California.

Not long after North Korea attacked South Korea and began to overrun the country, Wiedhahn again found himself on a troop ship, this time headed for the Pusan perimeter of Korea. The situation was desperate for the ROK, and the Marines were needed to stop the onslaught and give General Douglas MacArthur time to prepare for his landing of the X Corps at Inchon, where he successfully pushed the North Korean Army rapidly north. With the war appearing to be all but over, MacArthur was predicting that "our boys will be home by Christmas."

Then, China entered the fray. With the 5th and 7th Marines completely surrounded by units of the PVA (People's Volunteer Army) and with supply routes cut off, forcing flying boxcars to drop ammunition, food, clothing, and medical supplies onto the frozen reservoir—about a third of which was salvaged—it took 17 days of grueling fighting before the Marines were able to break through the encirclement. U.S. losses in dead, wounded, and missing totaled almost 18,000, while that of the enemy exceeded 48,000.

In 1953, then-staff sergeant Wiedhahn was commissioned a second lieutenant and after going through Basic Officers School at Quantico, Virginia, and a stint in Kodiak, Alaska, he went back to Camp Pendleton. In 1968, he was sent to Vietnam, where he was promoted to major and was the executive officer of the 3rd Battalion, 9th Marines. During his yearlong tour in Nam, he fought heroically in a number of battles, including Hue City, Operation Dewey Canyon, and Khe Sanh.

After his unit was pulled out, Wiedhahn was sent to Okinawa. He subsequently held various posts throughout the Marine Corps, including in the Office of Assistant Chief of Staff, G-4 (Logistics) at Headquarters Marine Corps in Washington, DC. Along the way, Wiedhahn received his promotion to colonel. All totaled, he spent 33 years in the Marines serving his country.

Today, Warren Wiedhahn is president of Military Historical Tours, Inc. in Alexandria, Virginia. He and his wife Jane reside in the neighboring community of Annandale.

"WHO WON THE WORLD SERIES?"

JACK YUSEN Veteran

"We will do our duty. The outcome is very doubtful."

Jack Yusen, recalling the announcement over the loudspeaker by the captain of the USS *Samuel B. Roberts* prior to the sinking of his ship by the Japanese, from an interview with *Veterans Chronicles*

The night sky on October 24, 1944, was filled with thunder and lighting. Or seemingly so. At the time, the battle was a long way off, with Admiral William Halsey's immense 3rd Fleet attacking the Japanese Center Force under Vice Admiral Takeo Kurita in the Sibuyan Sea. As Kurita pulled back, appearing to retreat, the Japanese plan was for the smaller Northern Force under Vice Admiral Takijirō Ōnisji to lure Halsey's battleships and carriers away from protecting the American forces landing on the island of Leyte in the Philippines. With Halsey in pursuit of Ōnisji, Kurita reversed direction and under the cover of darkness, his five battleships and a flotilla of cruisers and destroyers charged down the San Bernardino Straight toward Leyte.

The USS *Samuel B. Roberts*, the destroyer escort whose gallant stand at the Battle of Samar helped prevent a Japanese attack on the amphibious invasion fleet off the island of Leyte, October 25, 1944.

Standing in Kurita's way was Taffy 3, a light force of escort carriers, destroyers, and destroyer escorts, including the USS *Samuel B. Roberts*. On board the *Roberts*, Seaman First Class Jack Yusen was awakened by the call to general quarters. As the men rushed to their battle stations, the ship began to lay a heavy screen of black smoke to obscure the carriers. Without question, however, the five-inch guns of the *Roberts* would be no match against the heavy-caliber 18-inch artillery of the Japanese battleships and the eight-inch guns of the cruisers.

Though still 18 miles away, the Japanese battleships opened up on the *Roberts* and the other ships in task force Taffy 3.

It took an "Uncle Sam Wants You" poster to spur Yusen into enlisting. "My uncle, who was in

World War I, had always told me if I want to go into the service, go into the Navy, and that's what I did." Born and raised in the Queens section of Long Island, New York, Yusen was through high school at 17 and working for Fairchild Aviation in New York City. He was coming out of the subway, saw the poster, and went directly to the nearest Navy recruiting office.

Yusen went to boot camp in Seneca, New York, at Samson Naval Base and was ultimately assigned to the *Samuel B. Roberts*, a newly built destroyer escort. "We were assigned to the Atlantic Fleet and had Atlantic camouflage. We met the USS *Ranger*, two other destroyers, and two fleet oilers, and we were going to take them to North Africa."

Seven or eight hours off the New England coast, a whale hit the ship, knocked the propeller off the port side, and bent the propeller shaft. The *Roberts* was forced to drop out of the task force and pull into Norfolk, Virginia, for repairs. Once the ship was ready to go back to sea, a decision was made that the *Roberts* would be used for convoy work in the Pacific instead of the Atlantic. In a sense, Yusen noted, "A whale changed our destiny."

Training in the Pacific for a couple of weeks, escorting convoys, and surviving a typhoon at sea, the *Roberts* was ordered to join an armada of some 600 ships supporting General Douglas MacArthur's landing of Allied forces on the beaches of the Philippines. "Our job was to keep the enemy planes and the submarines away from our carriers."

What Yusen and his shipmates didn't realize was that the *Samuel B. Roberts* was headed for a rendezvous with Admiral Kurita and the main Japanese fleet. Suddenly, at a quarter to seven in the morning of October 25th, a host of enemy ships appeared on the horizon.

For three hours, the *Roberts* held its own against the Japanese fleet by positioning itself close to the Japanese cruisers so that the eight-inch guns on the cruisers couldn't be lowered enough to damage the ship. Meanwhile, the five-inch artillery of the *Roberts* was making hits on the bridge areas and exposed guns. But, eventually, a shell from one of the Japanese battleships plunged into the *Roberts* at the waterline, and the order came from Captain Robert Copeland to abandon ship.

Yusen and those able to make it off the ship jumped into the oily water, made it to rafts which they tied together, and watched the *Roberts* disappear, bow up, into the depths of the Pacific. For 72 hours, they floated with sharks swimming around them, pressing against the legs of those tied to the sides of the rafts. While the oil discouraged the sharks, "a shark took the leg off of a guy two down from me," Yusen recalled. Finally, a patrol boat showed up, but the survivors were so covered with the oil that they weren't recognizable.

Seaman First Class Jack R. Yusen

"Who are you?"

"*Samuel B. Roberts*."

"Who won the World Series?"

"St. Louis Cardinals."

"That's how we got saved," recalled Yusen.

Jack Yusen lives in Issaquah, Washington. Married for 62 years, he lost his wife Ruth in November 2011.

APPENDIX

Veterans Profiled in this Book Who Have Received America's Highest Military Awards

David Bellavia
Silver Star

Jacksel Broughton
Air Force Cross, Silver Star (2)

Roscoe Brown
Awarded the Congressional Gold Medal as member of Tuskegee Airmen

Frank Caldwell
Navy Cross

Lynn "Buck" Compton
Silver Star

Roger H. C. Donlon
Medal of Honor

Walter Ehlers
Medal of Honor

William Guarnere
Silver Star

Elaine Danforth Harmon
Awarded the Congressional Gold Medal as member of WASP

Thomas Hudner, Jr.
Medal of Honor

James Kanaya
Silver Star

Leonard Lomell
Distinguished Service Cross, Silver Star

Walker "Bud" Mahurin
Distinguished Service Cross, Silver Star

Joseph Walter Marm
Medal of Honor

Marco Martinez
Navy Cross

Thomas Moorer
Silver Star

James Morehead
Distinguished Service Cross (2), Silver Star

Mitchell Paige
Medal of Honor

Richard Stephen "Steve" Ritchie
Air Force Cross, Silver Star (4)

Dave Severance
Silver Star

Edward Shames
Silver Star

John Singlaub
Silver Star

Calvin Spann
Awarded the Congressional Gold Medal as member of Tuskegee Airmen

David Thatcher
Silver Star

William Tomlin
Silver Star

Theodore "Dutch" Van Kirk
Silver Star

Warren Wiedhahn
Silver Star